MARCH 2023

POWERING RECOVERY

Reform, Reconstruction, *and* Renewables *in* Conflict-Affected States *in the* Arab World

Foreword by
Jon B. Alterman

AUTHOR
Will Todman

CONTRIBUTING AUTHOR
Lubna Yousef

A Report of the
CSIS Middle East Program

ROWMAN & LITTLEFIELD

CSIS | CENTER FOR STRATEGIC & INTERNATIONAL STUDIES

ABOUT CSIS

The Center for Strategic and International Studies (CSIS) is a bipartisan, nonprofit policy research organization dedicated to advancing practical ideas to address the world's greatest challenges.

Thomas J. Pritzker was named chairman of the CSIS Board of Trustees in 2015, succeeding former U.S. senator Sam Nunn (D-GA). Founded in 1962, CSIS is led by John J. Hamre, who has served as president and chief executive officer since 2000.

CSIS's purpose is to define the future of national security. We are guided by a distinct set of values—nonpartisanship, independent thought, innovative thinking, cross-disciplinary scholarship, integrity and professionalism, and talent development. CSIS's values work in concert toward the goal of making real-world impact.

CSIS scholars bring their policy expertise, judgment, and robust networks to their research, analysis, and recommendations. We organize conferences, publish, lecture, and make media appearances that aim to increase the knowledge, awareness, and salience of policy issues with relevant stakeholders and the interested public.

CSIS has impact when our research helps to inform the decisionmaking of key policymakers and the thinking of key influencers. We work toward a vision of a safer and more prosperous world.

CSIS does not take specific policy positions; accordingly, all views expressed herein should be understood to be solely those of the author(s).

ISBN: 978-1-5381-7062-5 (pb); 978-1-5381-7063-2 (eBook)

Center for Strategic & International Studies
1616 Rhode Island Avenue, NW
Washington, DC 20036
202-887-0200 | www.csis.org

Rowman & Littlefield
4501 Forbes Boulevard
Lanham, MD 20706
301-459-3366 | www.rowman.com

ACKNOWLEDGMENTS

The authors would like to express their thanks to the many experts, policymakers, and practitioners in Iraq, Lebanon, Libya, Qatar, and Yemen who shared their knowledge, insights, and experience. The authors are also grateful to the experts in the United States, Europe, and the broader Middle East who generously shared their insights through remote interviews.

The authors are grateful to a remarkable collection of scholars and practitioners who helped shape this work by serving on its advisory board:

Prof. Sultan Barakat, Professor of Public Policy, Hamad bin Khalifa University

Amb. Frederick Barton, Lecturer of Public and International Affairs, Princeton University; former Assistant Secretary of State for Conflict and Stabilization Operations, U.S. Department of State

Prof. Melani Cammett, Clarence Dillon Professor of International Affairs, Department of Government, Harvard University; Chair of the Harvard Academy of International and Area Studies

Joel Charny, former Executive Director of Norwegian Refugee Council – USA

Helen Lackner, Visiting Fellow, European Council for Foreign Relations

Prof. Ellen Lust, Director of the Governance and Local Development Institute, University of Gothenburg

Dr. Michael Mason, Director of the Middle East Centre, London School of Economics and Political Science (LSE)

Dr. Robert Springborg, Non-resident Senior Fellow, Italian Institute of International Affairs; Adjunct Fellow, Simon Fraser University

Sahar Tabaja, Global Practice Lead, Peace, Stability, and Transition, Chemonics International

Michael Talhami, Regional Water and Habitat Adviser for the Near and Middle East, International Committee of the Red Cross (ICRC)

Each brought many decades of experience, and their wisdom was as inspiring as it was daunting. We are grateful to them for their guidance and ongoing enthusiasm for the project. While we are deeply grateful for their guidance, they bear no responsibility for our mistakes.

The authors are especially grateful to Dr. Jon Alterman, senior vice president, Zbigniew Brzezinski Chair in Global Security and Geostrategy, and director of the Middle East Program at CSIS, for his strategic guidance throughout the project. His encouragement, experience, and insight transformed this report. Natasha Hall also provided invaluable feedback on the draft.

The authors are also very grateful to the broader CSIS Middle East Program research team—Danny Sharp, Caleb Harper, and Mennah Abdelwahab provided extensive support—and we are grateful for the research efforts of former interns Soukayna Lakhsassi, Fiona Leary, Will McChesney, Kobe Spells, and Azim Wazeer.

The authors would also like to express their gratitude to Phillip Meylan and the team at the CSIS iDeas Lab, in particular Jeeah Lee and Leena Marte, whose production and design expertise has enriched the final product.

Finally, the authors would like to express their thanks to Ambassador Meshal bin Hamad Al Thani, Sheikh Abdulaziz Al Thani, and the Embassy of the State of Qatar, which supported this project. The shape of this project, as well as the opinions, conclusions, and recommendations expressed in its findings are those of the authors alone, and they do not represent the views of the embassy or the government of Qatar, which neither reviewed the project's findings nor provided any input to them before publication.

Any errors are the authors' alone.

ABBREVIATIONS

3RF	Lebanon Reform, Recovery and Reconstruction Framework
Ah	Ampere-hour
AFESD	Arab Fund for Economic and Social Development
CBL	Central Bank of Libya
CEDRE	Economic Conference for Development through Reforms with the Private Sector (Lebanon)
COP	Conference of the Parties (UN Climate Change Conference)
CPA	Coalition Provisional Authority (Iraq)
DRE	Distributed Renewable Energy
EDL	Electricité du Liban
EDZ	Electricité de Zahle
ERA	Electricity Regulatory Authority
GCCIA	Gulf Cooperation Council Interconnection Authority
GE	General Electric
GECOL	General Electricity Company of Libya
GMMR	Great Man-Made River (Libya)
GNA	Government of National Accord (Libya)
GNU	Government of National Unity (Libya)
GW	Gigawatt
IEA	International Energy Agency
IFI	International financial institution
IMF	International Monetary Fund
IOM	International Organization for Migration
INARA	Innovation for Affordable and Renewable Energy for All (Lebanon)

INGO	International nongovernmental organization
IRG	Internationally Recognized Government (Yemen)
ISG	Islamic State group
KRG	Kurdistan Regional Government (Iraq)
kWh	Kilowatt hour
LAB	Libyan Audit Bureau
LCEC	Lebanese Center for Energy Conservation
LFRE	Lebanese Foundation for Renewable Energy
LNA	Libyan National Army
MENA	Middle East and North Africa
MEW	Ministry of Energy and Water Resources (Lebanon)
MNC	Multinational corporation
MoEE	Ministry of Electricity and Energy (Yemen)
MW	Megawatt
NGO	Nongovernmental organization
NOC	National Oil Corporation (Libya)
PEC	Public Electricity Corporation (Yemen)
REAoL	Renewable Energy Agency of Libya
SIGIR	Special Inspector General for Iraq Reconstruction
UNDP	United Nations Development Programme
USAID	United States Agency for International Development
TWh	Terawatt hour

CONTENTS

FOREWORD

Having gained so much experience working in conflict-affected environments in the Middle East in recent decades, one would think the United States and its international partners would be enjoying great success. Together, these governments committed tens of billions of dollars to humanitarian relief, reconstruction, and peacebuilding.

Yet, few would argue that progress has been as dramatic as the donors had hoped. If we think critically about the failings of foreign assistance, one important element has been that after the fighting stopped, warlords and corruption became entrenched. Unscrupulous actors transitioned from the privileged positions they had during wartime to enjoy privileged positions in peacetime. Guns fell silent, but the financiers and militia leaders who prosecuted the war dug themselves in even more deeply.

Some of that is probably unavoidable; combatants need incentives to lay down their arms. But leaving combatants to monopolize service provision as the spoils of war, extracting wealth and dispensing patronage along the way, more deeply embeds the patterns of exploitation, marginalization, and oppression that led to conflict in the first place.

This excellent study by Will Todman provides a hint of how renewable energy offers a pathway toward a different outcome. He argues that small solar installations in conflict-affected environments allow economies to begin early recovery from war, empower local community leaders, and encourage self-sufficiency. Donors can implement these more modest efforts long before it is safe to make multimillion-dollar investments. In so doing, they help revive communities and grow their resilience before monopolists have a chance to sweep in. In fact, in today's war-torn communities, entrepreneurs are already implementing tiny solar projects. Donor interventions like the ones described here would amplify these efforts and scale up their impacts.

An added benefit, of course, is these projects would help conflict-affected countries accelerate the energy transition. Climate change disproportionately affects the Middle East, raising temperatures and dropping the water table even further. Clean energy not only contributes to global climate goals, but also helps promote the survivability of communities in a hostile climate.

Policy debates in Washington often occur at a very high level, and the personal experiences of individuals often get lost in the thrust and parry of large state actors competing for influence. Donors seeking dramatic change embrace multihundred-million-dollar projects with tens of thousands of beneficiaries. This paper presents a compelling argument for how impressively small things can grow and how broad their impact can be.

The strategies suggested here are still preliminary and need to be fine-tuned, but their promise is a strong justification for much greater donor exploration and experimentation than there has been up to now. These strategies are not a panacea, and they will not work everywhere. But once you have read this study, it will be hard to imagine not considering them.

Jon B. Alterman

Senior Vice President, Zbigniew Brzezinski Chair in Global Security and Geostrategy, Director, Middle East Program

EXECUTIVE SUMMARY

Donor efforts to tackle electricity crises in conflict-affected states in the Middle East have failed. Despite billions of dollars of international support for electricity infrastructure in Iraq, Lebanon, Libya, and Yemen, their electricity crises worsen year on year.

Multimillion-dollar thermal power stations created major and ongoing opportunities for graft and corruption, produced dangerous single points of electricity sector failure, and tied societies to future hydrocarbon use, undermining the energy transition. Many of these stations do not operate today.

Meanwhile, local political elites have successfully resisted reform demands from donors, the other traditional pillar of their electricity sector strategies. Donors often fail to appreciate that deficiencies in electricity provision in conflict-affected environments serve some elites' interests. When power outages are common, elites can secure the loyalty of key constituencies by providing them with preferential access to state power. Similarly, elites can profit by forcing communities to rely on expensive informal systems of electricity provision. These actors have a deep-seated interest in prolonging dysfunction in the electricity sector so that they can continue to profit, reward allies, and undermine rivals.

To tackle electricity crises in conflict-affected states, donors must take inspiration from local adaptations, think more politically, and act more quickly.

Advances in renewable energy technology are creating unprecedented opportunities. When national grids collapse during conflict, many communities turn to renewables as their primary alternative. Distributed systems of renewable electricity generation are not only better for the natural environment, but they also have specific advantages for fragile contexts.

To begin with, the consequences of destruction or debilitation of infrastructure are more contained in a distributed system, as outages affect a smaller area. Distributed systems also generate electricity closer to where it is consumed, and shorter transmission lines are more secure and reduce losses. The incorporation of renewable technologies into these systems reduces reliance on imports of fuel, which can often be disrupted during conflicts. Small-scale systems such as mini-grids can also be constructed more quickly than large-scale infrastructure.

Even more importantly, distributed systems of renewable electricity generation reduce opportunities for aspiring monopolists to gain business and influence. Decentralized systems have distributed ownership and involve smaller investments, making them a less attractive target for those seeking to profit from large aid contracts.

The danger is in waiting too long, as the experiences of Lebanon and Iraq highlight. Political elites in both countries have worked together to obstruct reforms that would limit their profits. For decades, the political classes in these countries have spent billions of dollars on electricity subsidies and conducted minimal tariff collection to prevent the entry of competitors into the electricity sector.

These experiences suggest that donors must act in the early recovery phase to advance an alternative system of electricity provision that can foster recovery and broader economic development. Distributed renewable energy technologies facilitate earlier donor interventions, which can yield much better longer-term outcomes. To seize advantage of a short-lived window of opportunity to deploy renewables, they must assess the capacity of local authorities and find ways to circumvent, co-opt, and coerce actors who benefit from the status quo. This assessment will determine the feasibility of interventions at the central and local levels.

At the central level, international donors should:

- condition support for central electricity infrastructure on reforms, such as establishing a legal framework for utility-scale and distributed renewable energy, an independent electricity regulator, and a tariff reform plan.
- support utility-scale renewable projects in more stable areas.
- avoid temporary fixes in the electricity sector that create new streams of income for aspiring monopolists, which could become permanent.

At the local level, donors should:

- assess local communities' openness and ability to partner with international actors.
- identify effective local adaptations that integrate renewable technologies and assess the reasons for their success and the feasibility of scaling them up.
- experiment with alternative systems of local electricity provision, including establishing mini-grids for rural communities and hybridizing preexisting neighborhood grids with solar panels.
- encourage private sector collaboration with local authorities, institutions, and communities to replicate and expand these systems.
- release feasibility studies and business models from successful initiatives.
- spread awareness of successful local initiatives nationally and with potential private sector investors.

KARAM AL-MASRI/AFP via Getty Images

INTRODUCTION

THE NEED FOR A NEW APPROACH

When the Syrian regime cut supplies of electricity and fuel to besieged Eastern Ghouta in 2013, bicycles emerged as an unlikely lifeline. Residents of the opposition-held enclave not only relied on bikes to travel around, but also to light up their homes: they paid young men to pedal bikes to generate electricity.[1]

The process was tiring and inefficient, but it provided enough power for the most basic needs. Charging one 14-ampere-hour (Ah) battery required around 40 minutes of continuous pedaling and cost the equivalent of $1.[2] That battery was enough to keep the lights on for several hours or to operate simple tools, but it could not pump water or run hospitals.

After trying several other innovations, a local council turned to solar energy. In 2014, they crowdfunded donations and then smuggled solar panels into the besieged area. A single panel was far more efficient than bike generation and could charge one 100 Ah battery each day. But some of the panels they installed on the roofs of schools were destroyed in bombings and others were stolen, leading local citizens to develop yet another workaround: converting burned-out vehicles into mobile solar generators by attaching solar panels.[3] These solar carts powered pumps to supply schools, mosques, and communal tanks with water.

Local innovations should inspire international donors to think differently about electricity crises in conflict-affected environments.[4] They demonstrate the possibility of implementing effective solutions at the community level that bring broader benefits, even in fragile contexts. Traditionally, donors avoid major interventions in the electricity sector while conflict conditions endure, and then make investments worth hundreds of millions of dollars when it is safe to do so. These investments often include major power plants and upgrades to state grids.

But in reintroducing massive power projects, donors bind societies to hydrocarbons and also close the door on adaptations that bloomed during periods of violence, including local experiments in renewable energy. This choice shuts the door on positive new innovations, levying costs that stretch beyond increased CO_2 emissions. The renewable energy economies that arise in many conflict-affected environments have unappreciated benefits, such as strengthening local governance and economies and hindering the emergence of new monopolists. The return to old ways of producing energy heightens the danger of slipping back into patterns of political economy that contributed to violence and inequalities in the first place. By contrast, retaining renewable innovations plants the seeds of broader recovery from conflict.

International donors could learn from some of the most promising local uses of renewable technology during conflicts and provide support to advance the diversification of the electricity sector. Earlier in the aftermath of a crisis than many might think, donors can seize upon a window of opportunity to build more resilient, sustainable, and equitable systems of electricity provision whose benefits extend far beyond the electricity sector.

AIMS AND METHODOLOGY

This report proposes a new approach for how international donors should assess electricity sector interventions in various types of conflict-affected environments. Analysis of four case studies helps evaluate the likely success of external interventions in different political and economic contexts. This report builds a typology of environments to highlight two critical factors. The first is central state capacity, which determines the viability of top-down or bottom-up interventions in the electricity sector. If authorities have limited capacity, local interventions are more appropriate. The second factor is the relative power of political and economic actors that have vested interests in the status quo. The strength of these interests is a critical factor that donors frequently underestimate. By identifying which actors benefit from the status quo and evaluating their influence, donors can better understand who could serve as spoilers to their efforts to improve electricity provision in conflict-affected environments. The report concludes with a rubric that proposes different courses of action donors should pursue in these distinct contexts, with an emphasis on the potential for renewables.

Further, this study explores the optimal time for international donors to intervene in electricity sectors in conflict-affected states, the types of interventions they should support, and which aims they should prioritize. It also highlights instances in which donors are unlikely to be impactful and should not pursue major interventions.

"

Donors can seize upon a window of opportunity to build more resilient, sustainable, and equitable systems of electricity provision whose benefits extend far beyond the electricity sector.

Politics are a central theme of the report. It explores how the political and economic interests of donors influence their interventions, the ways in which local politics constrain interventions, and the degree to which donor interventions have the potential to reshape local politics.

The study also considers if and when environmentally sustainable technologies create new opportunities for donor interventions in these contexts. It assesses the feasibility of donors pushing renewable technologies, given actors' economic and political interests in hydrocarbons and local politics, and what the political consequences of advancing such technologies in these contexts may be.

The study focuses on conflict-affected states. More than a third of states in the Middle East and North Africa (MENA) region currently experience fragility, conflict, and violence, and these crises are increasingly protracted.[5] The average length of war around the world has tripled since 2005.[6] To better understand donors' obstacles and opportunities at different stages of crisis, this study investigates a range of current and historic crises in Iraq, Lebanon, Libya, and Yemen.

These four countries are at different stages of armed conflict. Neither Iraq nor Lebanon experiences widespread violence today but do remain fragile. Lebanon's civil war ended three decades ago, and Iraq declared victory over the Islamic State Group (ISG) in 2017. Meanwhile, war continues in Libya and Yemen. The four countries also have disparate economies: Yemen is the poorest state in the MENA region and 80 percent of Lebanese live in poverty, but Libya and

Iraq enjoy substantial hydrocarbon wealth and upper-middle-income status. These four countries have also received varying levels of donor interest. Iraq received tens of billions of dollars of international assistance, while Libya has received comparatively little donor support or attention. These four countries also feature very different geography, from Iraq's largely flat expanses to Yemen's mountainous terrain and large rural populations. These factors mean that the electricity infrastructure in each country was very different before the conflicts, incurred different levels of destruction and disruption during conflict, and has different prospects for recovery.

This report relies on data gathered from a literature review, donor project databases, and interviews with more than 170 individuals across the four countries. Interviewees include state and local government officials, international donor officials and their implementing partners, local and international nongovernmental organization (NGO) workers, private sector actors, experts, and activists. CSIS also hired a consultant to conduct additional interviews in Yemen. The authors have anonymized the names of most interviewees to allow them to speak more freely. The authors conducted most interviews in Arabic and English, with some also conducted in French and Spanish.

A senior-level advisory board provided strategic guidance. The board consists of former government officials, leading academics, and practitioners who have decades of experience working on international humanitarian and development responses in the four case study countries and beyond.

THE TRADITIONAL APPROACH

International donors have spent billions of dollars trying to improve electricity provision in MENA states that have experienced war in recent decades.[7] Most of that investment has come long after fighting has ended. During conflicts, donors usually restrict their support to critical humanitarian service infrastructure, such as water pumping stations and medical facilities. They often provide fuel, backup generators, and some technical support to allow this infrastructure to continue to provide emergency services for populations. These efforts are piecemeal and largely uncoordinated—the United Nations' humanitarian coordination system does not include energy as a cluster or a cross-cutting theme. Even limited interventions face various obstacles. In addition to the ongoing threat of violence and the logistical challenges of accessing conflict-affected environments, donors must also navigate sanctions on individuals and groups, which limits their freedom of action.

When the dust has settled and most fighting has ended, donors pursue large interventions to support the reconstruction and rehabilitation of state electricity infrastructure. They often fall back on a familiar playbook and work on a few big projects. They contract to global energy companies to build or restore major hydrocarbon-fueled power stations and repair existing transmission and distribution lines. The main Western competitors for these contracts are General Electric (GE) and Siemens, which are supported by the U.S. and German governments, respectively. In Iraq, the two companies are competing for power contracts worth $15 billion.[8] In Yemen, Siemens built the country's largest power plant in Marib and recently signed a memorandum of understanding with the Yemeni government to rehabilitate and strengthen the country's infrastructure.[9] In both Yemen and Libya, GE has collaborated with Turkish contractor Çalık Enerji to supply gas turbine generators. GE and Siemens also collaborated with donors to submit offers to the Lebanese government in 2022 to supply electricity to Lebanon, although these have not moved forward.[10]

Large electricity projects have several advantages. One is that they can affect the lives of millions of beneficiaries in a single stroke. Another is that they require a finite set of high-value contracts with a limited number of counterparts, which makes the projects easier for the implementer to negotiate and monitor.

But the current patterns of rebuilding electricity supplies have failed to ensure reliable or affordable supplies of electricity in any MENA country that has experienced conflict in recent decades. Major donor-funded power stations in several conflict-affected states are idle. In early 2023, the Baiji power plant in Iraq, the Zahrani power plant in Lebanon, and the Marib power plant in Yemen are all offline because of destruction, insecurity, or economic crisis.

These large contracts contain false economies of scale. Not only do they tie countries to future hydrocarbon use and create single points of failure that malign actors can exploit, but many of them entrench poor governance. As electricity infrastructure is slowly rebuilt, warlords and criminal networks have used the construction of that infrastructure to cement the control they began building during wartime. These actors work to profit from lucrative fuel imports, secure commissions on major power contracts, and maintain the ability to reward their allies with preferential power provision. At the same time, elites have frustrated external efforts to induce reform or implement projects as specified. Successive Lebanese governments have failed to implement a law calling for an independent electricity regulatory authority for more than 20 years; the Iraqi parliament has failed to pass a law to facilitate the integration of renewable energy; and the Libyan state utility continues to grant multimillion-dollar contracts to major energy companies, despite previous contracts remaining incomplete. Political elites in conflict-affected states often believe that reforms would undercut their political and economic interests, and they favor ongoing weakness in the sector.

In this way, spending on electricity programs has worked at cross-purposes with democracy and governance programs, a mainstay of Western donor interest. Western governments use these programs to help stamp out corruption, yet many of their big projects fuel the very corruption they are seeking to eliminate. Instead, political elites across the region have profited richly from international electricity funding, through kickbacks, bribes, and racketeering in the electricity sector.

The consequences of failing to address electricity crises in conflict-affected states will only grow in the years to come. The energy transition underway around the world will eventually force all states that rely on hydrocarbons for electricity production to reconstruct their electricity sectors entirely. Meanwhile, ongoing population growth, urbanization, and the effects of climate change will exert unprecedented strain on electricity networks.

Donors must reflect on the ineffectiveness of their interventions and the success of local adaptations. Rather than reconstructing old infrastructure, donors should pursue opportunities to make the electricity sector more reliable, more resilient to future shocks, and more resistant to elite capture. Drawing inspiration from local initiatives would allow them to do so. Local communities often find ways to navigate the political, economic, and logistical obstacles of conflict-affected environments to develop their own means of providing electricity. The benefits of boosting these initiatives could extend far beyond the electricity sector, laying the ground for economic recovery, environmental sustainability, and peacebuilding.

"

Political elites across the region have profited richly from international electricity funding, through kickbacks, bribes, and racketeering in the electricity sector.

Wathiq Khuzaie/Getty Images

CONFLICT, PROFIT, AND RENEWABLES

External actors seeking to improve electricity provision in conflict-affected states must investigate the shifting politics of the sector, changing access to economic opportunities, and which actors benefit from poor state electricity provision. Disruptions in the electricity sector create new streams of profit, electricity provision can become a tool of war, and grievances about power shortages can drive conflict.

By destroying infrastructure, disrupting the import of fuel and other necessary inputs, and displacing critical personnel, conflicts tend to fragment the electricity sector. State monopolies often collapse, and local adaptations fill the void.

These adaptations can create new winners, such as neighborhood generator owners in Lebanon and Iraq, who gain new streams of income and influence.[11] Over time, political elites work to cement relationships with these private actors and to secure a portion of the profits.

Electricity access is often used as a weapon of war. In conflicts across the MENA region and beyond, armed actors have weaponized electricity access, destroying key infrastructure and limiting electricity provision to undermine their adversaries. The ISG destroyed Iraq's largest power station and has conducted dozens of attacks on transmission lines to undermine the Iraqi state. Likewise, Libyan militias that control electricity infrastructure have disrupted supplies of electricity to exert leverage over their rivals. These tactics are playing out beyond the Middle East as well. Russia destroyed 30 percent of Ukraine's power stations in October 2022 alone, causing blackouts across much of the country.[12]

Uneven electricity access serves as a driver of conflict and plants the seeds for future instability. Lebanon's political class prioritized Beirut in the post-war reconstruction process and provided it with greater access to state electricity than peripheral areas, marginalizing Lebanese outside the capital. In southern Iraq, the acute weakness of the electricity sector provokes annual protests. In southern Libya, residents of a small town cut the capital's access to water to protest long power cuts in 2019.

Donors often fail to appreciate that deficiencies in electricity provision in conflict-affected environments serve some elites' interests. When power outages are common, elites can secure the loyalty of key constituencies and integrate economic actors into patronage networks by providing them with preferential access to state power. Similarly, elites can profit by forcing communities to rely on expensive informal systems of electricity provision. These actors have a deep-seated interest in ensuring the continuation of the status quo in the electricity sector so that they can continue to profit, reward allies, and undermine rivals. Therefore, many long-term electricity crises in conflict-affected states are deliberate.

"

Donors often fail to appreciate that deficiencies in electricity provision in conflict-affected environments serve some elites' interests.

THE PROMISE OF RENEWABLES

Any electricity intervention in a conflict-affected environment must grapple with these political and economic interests. The solution to deliberate electricity crises is for donors to find other ways to provide power, not to refrain from intervening at all.

Advances in renewable energy technology are creating unprecedented opportunities for navigating the politics of electricity provision in conflict-affected countries. Utility-scale renewable technology is now cost competitive with, or even cheaper than, conventional electricity infrastructure in many cases and should be advanced when feasible in more stable regions.[13] However, central authorities must have significant capacity to create a conducive environment for these projects, attract financing, and secure them.

But distributed systems of renewable electricity generation can be implemented even when instability remains and central capacity is weak. Unlike centralized generation through large power stations, distributed systems of electricity generation rely on smaller-scale infrastructure that allows electricity to be generated close to where it is consumed. Renewable or hybrid mini-grids (e.g., for neighborhoods, institutions, and industries) and sludge-to-energy systems have specific advantages in more challenging security, economic, and political contexts, in addition to their benefits for the natural environment.

Distributed systems increase the resilience of electricity infrastructure.[14] The consequences of the destruction or debilitation of infrastructure are more contained in a distributed system, as outages are confined to a smaller area. Likewise, electricity is generated closer to where it is consumed. The shorter transmission lines involved in such systems are more secure and reduce losses, while communities are more likely to support and protect local infrastructure that clearly serves them. These systems can also incorporate renewable technologies to reduce reliance on regular imports of fuel, which can often be disrupted during conflicts. Hybrid systems, which combine renewable technologies and gas- or diesel-fueled generators, further increase resilience by limiting single points of failure.

Distributed systems also provide broader benefits in conflict-affected environments. Small-scale projects such as mini-grids can be constructed more quickly than large-scale infrastructure. Rapidly providing electricity access accelerates local economic development and job creation and reduces grievances about poor-quality services, which are often drivers of conflict. Mini-grids likewise rely on local ownership, which capitalizes on extant social capital in contexts characterized by a general lack of trust in authority. In many conflict-affected environments, solidarity remains high among local communities while trust in the state's ability to provide essential services falls. Furthermore, distributed systems that integrate renewable technology reduce the reliance on toxic diesel generators, bringing health and environmental advantages, and incorporate metering systems that can help rationalize energy consumption and deter wasteful behavior.[15] And in the longer term, advancing the deployment of renewable technologies helps cushion MENA societies from future disruptions due to the energy transition.

Perhaps most importantly, distributed systems of renewable electricity generation reduce opportunities for aspiring monopolists to gain business and influence. Decentralized systems have distributed ownership, making it harder for corrupt groups to exercise wide-reaching control. Although local capture is still possible, these systems involve smaller investments, making them less attractive for those seeking to profit from large aid contracts. And by reducing the electricity sector's reliance on fuel imports, distributed systems limit another activity which is often highly profitable for corrupt actors.

However, these systems require high-quality equipment and sufficient technical expertise to install and maintain. In many conflict-affected environments, assuring the quality of imported equipment is challenging. Donors should only contract with trusted companies that maintain high standards, as funding low-quality equipment would undermine communities' trust in the new technology. Donors should also ensure that training programs are embedded in these projects.[16]

To be sure, these renewable systems are not a silver bullet for electricity provision in all conflict-affected states in the MENA region, but they show promise in key contexts. Donors must carefully explore the politics of electricity sectors in each state to identify opportunities and tailor solutions to specific states and communities. They should focus on an evaluation of the capacity of central authorities and the influence of actors that profit from the status quo in the electricity sector.

IRAQ SQUANDERED OPPORTUNITIES

After decades of instability following the U.S.-led invasion of Iraq in 2003 and the rise of the ISG, security has greatly improved in many parts of Iraq, but the situation remains precarious for electricity pylons.

ISG cells claimed responsibility for more than 60 attacks on electricity towers across Iraq in the summer of 2021, which left millions without power during a heatwave.[17] But some Iraqi politicians suspected others were responsible.

Iraqi member of parliament Falah Abdul-Karim al-Khafaji blamed "political parties with armed cells," that were seeking to undermine the government of Mustafa al-Kadhimi in the run-up to elections, a thinly veiled reference to Iran-backed militias.[18] Others suspected private generator owners were responsible, as their revenues increased when state electricity provision declined.[19] In reality, it could have been any number of different actors. More groups seem to have an interest in undermining the state-led electricity sector in Iraq than supporting it.

"

More groups seem to have an interest in undermining the state-led electricity sector in Iraq than supporting it.

Iraq's electricity sector is a story of squandered opportunities. Decades of conflict and sanctions have inflicted heavy costs on Iraqis, but the country is better placed to establish reliable state electricity than other conflict-affected states in the region for several reasons. First, Iraq is a middle-income country with the fifth-largest proven hydrocarbon reserves in the world. It has both substantial government revenues and large domestic sources of fuel. Second, Iraq has enjoyed a higher level of donor interest than any other conflict-affected state. International actors have spent billions of dollars to improve electricity provision over the past two decades. Third, Iraq's geography helps electricity provision. The country is largely flat, and there are few areas that are not connected to the national grid. Finally, Iraq has the potential for a highly resilient grid, with conditions that allow for significant hydro, wind, and solar installations.

Yet, Iraq and international donors have squandered these advantages, and the window of opportunity to rebuild the electricity sector to be more resilient and efficient and to instill better governance has now closed. Inside Iraq, political factions often seek kickbacks from state electricity projects and profit from informal electricity provision due to their close ties to neighborhood generator owners. External actors also have interests in Iraq's electricity sector. For example, Iran seeks to keep Iraq dependent on electricity and gas imports from Iran, and it instrumentalizes that dependence for political gain. Western donors have also sought to advance the interests of multinational corporations (MNCs), such as GE and Siemens, at the expense of improving the resilience of the sector. Although Iraq has relatively strong central government capacity in comparison to other conflict-affected states, so many actors have a stake in dysfunction that belated efforts to advance renewables have little chance of success.

Over more than five decades, Iraqis have learned to expect cheap and plentiful state electricity. Yet, Iraq's deep oil reserves have meant the electricity sector has remained inefficient. The government continues to bankroll billions of dollars of losses every year in the electricity sector, including subsidies, uncollected bills, and illegal connections.[20] That pattern squanders state finances and deters competition. When Saddam Hussein fell, donors did little to incentivize reforms and increase the resilience of the electricity sector. Now, parties that favor the status quo have dug in and effectively limit the ability of donors to effect change.

Major Electricity Infrastructure in Iraq

Source: Adapted from Robin Mills and Maryam Salman, "Powering Iraq: Challenges Facing the Electricity Sector in Iraq" Al-Bayan Center for Planning and Studies, October 2020, 19, https://library.fes.de/pdf-files/bueros/amman/16923.pdf.

RECONSTRUCTION

In the late twentieth century, the Iran-Iraq war, the Gulf War, and international sanctions all downgraded Iraq's electricity sector.[21] Damage to electricity infrastructure during the Gulf War caused electricity production to drop from 3,100 megawatts (MW) per day to below 2,200 MW, and the international sanctions regime complicated Saddam Hussein's ability to import the necessary parts to maintain and rebuild energy infrastructure.[22]

Conflicts in the twenty-first century caused far more substantial damage. In the immediate aftermath of the U.S.-led 2003 invasion, electricity production fell from 4,000 MW per day to just 500 MW per day, and reconstruction of the electricity sector was severely delayed.[23] The Coalition Provisional Authority (CPA) aimed to reach 6,000 MW of generation capacity by the middle of 2004, but it took until 2011 to reach that target.[24]

Donors demonstrated little commitment to building back better when it came to Iraq's electricity sector. Reconstruction activities focused on increasing generation capacity, but they failed to build resilience in the electricity sector or tackle the sector's underlying governance issues. Likewise, the CPA missed opportunities to incorporate Iraqis into the process. In total, the United

States spent more than $5 billion dollars on the reconstruction of the electricity sector between 2003 and 2012. The final Special Inspector General for Iraq Reconstruction (SIGIR) report criticized the focus on large-scale electricity projects, which created single points of failure and were vulnerable to attacks.

Unsurprisingly, U.S.-led reconstruction in the electricity sector failed to meet Iraqis' expectations. Locals knew that billions of dollars were being spent on power infrastructure, but the restoration of electricity service to pre-invasion levels took far longer than anticipated, and Iraqis felt cut out of the process. Few Iraqis were involved in decisionmaking, and few benefited from employment. Furthermore, the U.S. government's shifting priorities diminished Iraqis' trust and stoked their grievances.[25] After a review in 2004, the United States reprogrammed $3 billion dollars away from the electricity and water sectors toward security and economic development.[26] In a 2011 survey, after most U.S. troops had withdrawn from Iraq, almost 80 percent of Iraqis rated electricity provision as "bad or very bad."[27]

> "
>
> **Donors demonstrated little commitment to building back better when it came to Iraq's electricity sector.**

More recently, ISG attacks are estimated to have caused at least $7 billion of damage to the power sector.[28] Their most impactful attack damaged Iraq's largest power station, at Baiji, which had only just opened. After the ISG's territorial defeat, donors deprioritized electricity again and failed to learn the lessons from post-Saddam reconstruction. They failed to take advantage of important advances in the efficiency and affordability of renewable technology. Integrating renewable technology more widely into Iraq's electricity system would have helped diversify the grid, made it more resilient to future periods of instability, improved local ownership, reduced carbon emissions, and reduced losses in the sector. As one UN official based in Baghdad remarked, "Donors never pushed us on renewables at all."[29] Instead, donors prioritized large projects and rebuilt the preexisting infrastructure.

The interests of MNCs also shaped reconstruction priorities. Energy companies had a strong incentive to reconstruct preexisting infrastructure rather than reimagine the Iraqi energy sector to be more efficient or more resilient to future shocks. New infrastructure projects would have opened new tender processes for billion-dollar contracts, which they did not want to risk losing.[30] In 2021, an Iraqi parliamentary commission called for an investigation into sole-source electricity contracts that the Iraqi government awarded to GE, Siemens, and others, citing allegations of corruption.[31]

THE CURRENT CRISIS

Given the status of Iraq's power sector, it is clear that the donor-led reconstruction process has been deeply flawed. Despite an estimated $81 billion spent on the electricity sector since 2005, outages in Iraq are the norm and are getting worse.[32] Demand increases by 7 to 10 percent each year and dramatically outstrips supply.[33] The supply-demand gap was 12 gigawatts (GW) in 2021, equivalent to 44 percent of available generation capacity.[34] Most Iraqis receive power only half the time. Outages increase during summer months when searing temperatures cause energy demand to peak. There are also regional disparities in electricity provision, with the worst outages consistently occurring in the oil-rich southern governorates.

Making matters even worse, the electricity sector is a significant financial burden for the Iraqi government. Energy subsidies cost the government an average of $6.5 million per day, or about 4 percent of Iraq's GDP.[35] Most Iraqis pay just a tenth of the true kilowatt hour (kWh) cost of electricity, and many pay nothing at all.[36] The incentives lead many Iraqis to be wasteful with their electricity consumption. A former electricity minister stated that he heard of Iraqis in Basra placing air conditioning units on balconies so that they could smoke shisha outside when state power is available, even in the height of summer.[37] Despite paying little to the state, Iraqis' overall electricity bills are high because they rely on expensive private generators. The International Energy Agency (IEA) estimated that generators captured annual revenues of around $4 billion in 2018.[38]

Iraq's electricity sector also has among the highest losses in the world.[39] Technical losses from low-quality transmission lines and distribution networks sap about 20 percent of output, and administrative losses—including illegal connections and unpaid bills—account for as much as another 40 percent.[40] The quality of the fuel Iraq uses to power turbines further exacerbates losses, as Iraq generally operates turbines with heavy fuel rather than gas, tripling the need for maintenance.[41]

The electricity crisis drives instability and stymies economic growth. The government provides preferential electricity access to certain critical institutions and "politically sensitive" areas, such as hospitals, clinics, and shrines, in an attempt to stem instability.[42] However, outages spark mass protests each year and have paralyzed cities and forced several electricity ministers to resign. Power cuts have shut down airports, undermined businesses, and stymied job creation. The IEA estimates that Iraq's inability to meet demand has lost $120 billion in jobs and industrial demand between 2014 and 2020.[43] Shortages of electricity also exacerbate Iraq's displacement crisis. Data from the International Organization for Migration (IOM) show that electricity issues are a significant barrier to the return of internally displaced people.[44]

THE KURDISTAN REGION OF IRAQ

"The sun is the center of our flag, of course we understand its importance!" a Kurdish official laughed. The Kurdistan Regional Government (KRG) manages its own electricity network and has worked to integrate renewable energy into the mix to a greater extent than federal Iraq. Today, it experiences shorter electricity outages than federal Iraq and has worked to create an enabling legal environment for private sector investment in the electricity sector.

Iraqi Kurdistan has long relied on renewables for electricity provision. It has two hydropower dams, built in the 1970s and 1980s, with a combined capacity of 650 MW. However, decreasing water levels and a lack of maintenance have reduced their output significantly to just 163 MW today. The KRG has also relied on the private sector for electricity provision, operating through independent power producers. The parliament recently approved the construction of two solar power plants in Dohuk and Erbil, each with an initial capacity of 25 MW and the potential for significant expansion.

The KRG has also laid the groundwork for private actors to pump solar power into the grid. At the domestic level, the government has installed more than 1.2 million smart meters for households across the Kurdistan Region of Iraq (KRI). These households receive credits for their energy bills if they export energy into the grid. The government is now working on the trickier process of defining a billing process for commercial actors. Budgetary constraints mean that the government has little ability to purchase electricity, which limits the expansion of solar power.

Because of its unique political status within Iraq, the KRG struggles to access international finance for expanding solar power. It cannot engage directly with the World Bank, and Kurdish officials said the administrative process for accessing green funds is too complicated. They bemoan donors' lack of coordination and their focus on short-term interventions. Kurdish officials have the vision, they argue, and are working to create the necessary legal environment for solar to take off—they just lack the resources to fully capitalize on the power of the sun.

Source: Author's interviews with Kurdish officials, Erbil, June 8, 2022.

STUMBLING REFORMS

The solutions to Iraq's electricity problems appear clear on paper, but the government has made insufficient efforts to implement them. As a first step, the government would have to find ways to end wasteful consumption, starting with lifting electricity and fuel subsidies and improving tariff collection. In 2016, under the premiership of Haidar al-Abbadi, the government experimented with pay-for-use schemes by installing billing systems in upper-middle-class neighborhoods in Baghdad, including Harthiya, Zayuna, and Yarmouk. These model neighborhood projects reduced consumption by two-thirds and provided uninterrupted electricity, but the projects attracted fierce political backlash.[45] Rumors and disinformation campaigns stoked anger about rising electricity bills. The experiments remain successful but have not been scaled up or replicated elsewhere.[46]

While higher tariffs remain unpopular, other reforms to reduce consumption would likely face less resistance. Increasing energy efficiency would lower energy costs for consumers and yield several additional benefits. For every $1 million invested in energy efficiency to retrofit buildings or to build new energy efficient buildings, the government could create an estimated 15 jobs and reduce buildings' energy usage by up to 90 percent.[47]

The government would also have to improve supplies of electricity. Successive governments have focused on increasing generation capacity, but other steps would be more effective. The most impactful intervention would be to end gas flaring—whereby gas is merely burned at oil wells as a byproduct of oil drilling—and to use captured natural gas for electricity generation.[48] Investing in repairs to the grid would be cheaper and would reduce technical losses substantially.

Iraq would also need to improve the governance of the sector to streamline decisionmaking, facilitate private sector involvement, and reduce opportunities for corruption. A key step would be to create an independent electricity regulator. Doing so could protect consumers from abuse by companies with significant market

Gas flaring in southern Iraq.

HUSSEIN FALEH/AFP via Getty Images

power, facilitate investment, and promote economic efficiency. Another way to attract investment into the sector would be to pass legislation that facilitates the wider integration of renewables into the energy mix.

Iraq has every incentive to diversify its energy mix, and renewables are an obvious solution. At present, Iraq relies on hydrocarbons for 98 percent of its electricity generation, which creates more than half of Iraq's total carbon emissions.[49] Iraq is acutely vulnerable to the effects of climate change. For example, it is quickly running out of water, extreme temperatures are rising as much as seven times faster than the global average, and it experiences dozens of debilitating dust and sandstorms each year, which are driven by increasing desertification.[50] Although Iraq bears little responsibility for global greenhouse gas emissions, it has various resources to reduce its carbon footprint.[51] As well as its hydropower and wind resources, Iraq is especially well suited for solar energy.

Iraq has squandered opportunities to tackle the building crisis and is only belatedly focusing on climate issues. Baghdad ratified the Kyoto Protocol 10 years after the initial signing period and only ratified its nationally determined contribution to the Paris Agreement in 2021, a full five years after the agreement went into effect. As a result, Iraq has missed out on important opportunities to use processes like the Clean Development Mechanism to promote environmentally responsible practices, such as capturing flared gas during oil extraction.[52] The 2021 UN Climate Change Conference in Glasgow (COP26) prompted a push toward renewables in Iraq, but senior ministers warn that progress is still not occurring at the "speed or scale you would expect."[53]

"

Iraq has squandered opportunities to tackle the building crisis and is only belatedly focusing on climate issues.

Political instability has frustrated the government's efforts to diversify its energy mix and reduce electricity consumption. The government had plans to increase the share of renewable energy to 20 percent by 2030, and the Ministry of Electricity held a pilot licensing round in July 2019 for independent power producers to develop solar power sites with a combined capacity of 750 MW.[54] The government also announced plans to reform electricity tariffs and remove subsidies in September 2019.[55] Weeks later, the October revolution brought these plans to an abrupt stop. As a result, the potential of utility-scale renewable energy remains untested. It is currently unclear if Iraq's grid can cope with the fluctuations in output from solar panels, the impact of dust storms on solar panels, or the true kWh cost of energy produced from solar panels in Iraq.

The underdevelopment of Iraq's private sector has prevented it from driving the renewable sector in the absence of government action. At least 30 new companies have entered Iraq's renewable energy market in recent years, but just five of them are medium-sized companies. One of the largest of these, Infinity Green Power, has installed an impressive 7.2 MW of capacity across Iraq.[56] But most of the solar companies have very small offices, and some are single engineers selling their own solar panels.[57] Smaller solar business owners struggle to make profits and end up acting more like environmental charities than businesses.[58] The Chinese solar module manufacturer LONGi is one example of prominent international companies in the renewable market and is working to expand its business in Iraq. However, the insufficient legal framework for renewable energy is an obstacle to more substantial private sector investment in renewable energy. Although the United Nations Development Programme (UNDP) provided the Iraqi government assistance in drafting a renewable energy law, it has not yet been submitted to parliament.

The lack of financing for renewables is also an important obstacle. The central bank of Iraq sought to address this problem by launching a 1 trillion Iraqi dinar ($680 million) fund to provide financing for solar technology in 2021. The program provides soft loans for different types of borrowers.[59] However, details of the program's implementation remain poorly defined, and private sector actors expressed varying levels of faith in the program.[60] Some firms complained that eligibility is unclear, that suppliers benefit little from the program, and that there are insufficient financial incentives for consumers, as monthly loan repayments are higher than most Iraqis pay for private generators. They also warned that it could become another vehicle for corruption, as some banks were setting up their own solar companies.[61] Bank managers could grant themselves loans from the central bank with little oversight, despite having no proven track record of successfully implementing solar projects.

Iraq also struggles from a lack of public receptivity to renewable energy. Iraq's oil wealth has helped create a belief that it is the government's duty to provide cheap electricity. Although many Iraqis have enough money to invest in renewables, this sense of entitlement deters them from doing so. "Iraqis would much prefer to upgrade their car than invest in more productive ways to improve their situation," a solar company owner in Mosul complained.[62] Confusion about technical details, disinformation, and the enduring damage caused by bad projects, such as the widely publicized failure of a solar-powered streetlight program, also undermine public receptibility. However, the greatest challenges to advancing renewable technology in Iraq are political.

KEEPING IRAQ'S SOLAR COMMUNITY ON MESSAGE

Amer al-Azaawy founded a small solar company in Baghdad. With little public awareness about the benefits of solar energy and no government support, his efforts felt futile. He decided that if the government was not going to act, he would take matters into his own hands. To do so, he created a WhatsApp group.

This group, the "Renewable Energy Forum," is a space for Iraqi academics, experts, policymakers, businesspeople, and investors from the diaspora to engage in a serious discussion about renewable energy in Iraq. The group's 249 members are carefully curated and share frequent updates, best practices, and opportunities to advance the cause. Al-Azaawy works hard to keep the members on message. "All good morning messages, pictures of flowers, and other niceties will be deleted," he warned. One member admitted that she often mutes notifications because the group is so active but also said she learns a lot whenever she tunes into the conversation.

The new virtual solar community proved so successful that al-Azaawy sought to build on it. He cofounded a new company under the same name with several members of the group. Although many of them are technically competitors, they know that collaboration is critical to kickstart the solar market in Iraq. They hope that they can attract serious investment to be able to work on more ambitious and impactful projects.

However, al-Azaawy is conscious that politics has a way of ruining promising initiatives in Iraq. He has taken several steps to protect the group from politicization. As well as refusing entry to foreign diplomats, he imposed a ban on any messages related to sectarianism, the violation of others' beliefs, or insults. Every morning, he quickly deletes several messages. It is never clear if the messages contained a political allegation or a GIF of sparkling roses.

Source: Author's interview with Amer al-Azaawy, Baghdad, June 6, 2022.

POLITICS AND VESTED INTERESTS

Opportunities to reform the electricity sector, which is rife with mismanagement and corruption, have often been squandered due to a lack of political will. Mass protests about electricity cuts have forced several electricity ministers to resign over the past decade, driving politicians to avoid reforms that might stoke discontent. High government turnover also frustrates reform agendas. Politicians seek ribbon-cutting ceremonies at new power stations to demonstrate progress to their constituents rather than pursuing needed reforms or making longer-term investments that will make a more substantial improvement.[63] One former minister of electricity equated the changing leadership of the sector with "constantly changing surgeons in the middle of a 10-hour surgery."[64] The reform imperative also declines when oil prices are high. The government postpones projects and stalls because it can afford inaction.[65]

Decisionmaking in the electricity sector is highly fragmented, with no single Iraqi authority empowered to direct the sector.[66] The sector is also subject to significant international influence, which shapes and constrains policymaking options. Donor governments, international financial institutions, and MNCs, including GE, Siemens, and Total, all play a large role. Regionally, Iran has important leverage because it exports both electricity and gas to Iraq. Gulf Arab states are also playing a growing role, with significant Emirati investment through Masdar and efforts to supply Iraq with electricity through the GCC Interconnection Authority (GCCIA). With multiple actors trying to pull electricity policy in different directions, the result is often stasis. As a solar business owner in Baghdad noted, "Whenever one faction makes a decision, the others work to block it."[67]

The electricity sector has become a cashflow generator for actors at different levels. At the highest level of government, billion-dollar contracts provide substantial opportunities for kickbacks. A former senior executive of an MNC said that there were so many vectors of corruption when negotiating a contract that he found it difficult to decipher what the government's actual policy was.[68] As well as government officials seeking benefits, political parties wield significant influence over contracting processes. Parties have employees inside ministries who feed them information about the details of contracts. The parties then offer to "unstick" the approval of contracts if MNCs cut them into the deal.[69]

MNCs are far from faultless. Because of their outsized influence in the market, MNCs often seek to shape government policies to their own advantage. For example, they often push the government to purchase more generation capacity rather than rehabilitating the grid. They see Iraq as one of the last markets in which they can install older gas turbines without facing pushback due to environmental concerns.[70] Both GE and Siemens have paid millions of dollars to settle civil claims with the U.S. Securities and Exchange Commission for violating bribery laws.[71]

On the local level, electricity officials collect bribes and private generator owners profit richly. The Ministry of Electricity sends its employees to cut illegal connections using specialized cranes, but Iraqis often bribe them to restore these connections.[72] Neighborhood generator owners also make substantial profits. They receive subsidized fuel from the government and then charge their customers high prices.[73] Customers complain that the frequency and voltage of power supplied by private generators are unstable, which can break appliances.[74] Despite the poor and expensive service, generator "cartels" often enjoy close links to political parties and have local monopolies.[75] Several political parties have interests in ensuring that Iraqis depend on private generators, as this business creates several revenue streams.

On the international level, Iran profits most from Iraq's dysfunctional electricity sector. Iraq relies on Iran for about 35 percent of its electricity supplies, either through gas or electricity imports.[76] Iran works to undermine efforts to end gas flaring, which would reduce Iraq's need for Iranian imports.[77] Iraq flares the second-largest amount of gas in the world, wasting an estimated $2.5 billion worth of gas per year, which could fuel 10 GW of electricity. Furthermore, gas flaring drives a public health crisis, as the practice is highly polluting and is tied to high rates of cancer.[78] Beyond Iran, oil companies also have an interest in flaring gas, as it is cheaper than capturing, processing, and marketing it.

These vested interests block most efforts to reform Iraq's electricity sector. A multitude of actors view the dysfunctional status quo as serving their economic and political interests.

> "Despite the poor and expensive service, generator "cartels" often enjoy close links to political parties and have local monopolies.

DONOR STRATEGIES

The challenging political environment has deterred donors from focusing on the electricity sector in recent years. Unlike the high degree of donor unity on post-ISG stabilization efforts, electricity has not been a major donor priority, and responses have been uncoordinated. Even in post-ISG reconstruction, donors have devoted very little focus to energy efficiency, despite its potential to reduce energy consumption dramatically. For example, a UN official working on post-ISG reconstruction said that most donors opted to fund the construction of standard housing units that were 30 percent cheaper than energy efficient units.[79]

In the absence of government support for reforms, donors are seeking opportunities at the local level. Several donors have determined that supporting private sector actors working in renewable energy is their most effective intervention. They hope that the private sector can drive market demand even if the government fails to act. Most Iraqi solar energy companies readily accept international funding, as it represents an important share of their revenues, given the limited domestic market for renewables. They also benefit from relationships with donors in other ways. For example, UN agencies have conducted effective training programs for businesses on marketing and reducing costs.[80] Several Western embassies are trying to facilitate the entry of renewable energy businesses from their countries in the Iraqi market. However, some larger international solar companies are unwilling to work with donor governments because of perceived reputational risk. They fear that projects with large budgets have limited impact because of the high cost of operations and overheads and therefore do not want to be associated with them.[81]

Donors have not enjoyed great success working with local authorities or generator owners. Because generator owners receive heavily subsidized fuel from the government and often have local monopolies, they have little financial incentive to hybridize their grids with solar power. It is challenging for donors to engage with generator owners, given their often opaque ties to political parties and armed groups. Some private sector actors have attempted to work with generator owners, but they have also had little success, saying they are often poorly educated and resistant to new ways of doing things.[82]

Some of the most successful donor interventions have been installing solar-powered water pumps for irrigation. Fuel is especially expensive in rural areas because companies charge more to transport it farther. These interventions are relatively cheap because the systems do not need to operate at night and so do not require expensive battery storage. There are also fewer veto holders in remote areas, and no actors have a strong incentive to block these kinds of projects. The United States Agency for International Development (USAID) and several other donors are working to expand access to financing for agricultural solar projects. UNDP implemented a project close to the border with Syria, far away from the grid, to prove that solar interventions are possible even in the most challenging environments.[83]

But remote areas far away from population centers are not the most challenging environments. Instead, the lack of progress that donors have made in urban areas suggests that these areas are far more challenging. Overall, donors have assessed that the political economy works against reform to such an extent that they would achieve little by attempting to push for change.

CONCLUSION: STRONG CENTRAL CAPACITY AND ENTRENCHED INTERESTS IN THE STATUS QUO

Iraq demonstrates the complex obstacles to introducing renewables into electrical systems as well as the dangers of squandering opportunities to improve systems when donors have the ability to do so. Donors spent billions of dollars to rebuild Iraq's electricity sector, but they failed to combine it with sufficient efforts to build resilience and improve governance. Although Iraq has enormous potential for renewable energy and a relatively strong central government, private interests, politics, and mismanagement have colluded to block it. These actors profit from the status quo in the electricity sector.

Iraq's electricity system is in crisis and now rife with corruption. The government is unable to implement reforms that would undercut the interests of powerful actors, including Iran, political parties, international companies, or private generator owners.

Although donor interventions are unlikely to bring about transformative change in Iraq's electricity sector, donors are squandering an opportunity by not placing more emphasis on renewable electricity. Donors should focus on discrete interventions that could accelerate the spread of renewables. They should exert collective pressure on parliament to pass the renewable energy law and to create an independent electricity regulator. Donors are often hesitant to wield this kind of pressure, but the power of their collective leverage in the electricity sector has been untested.

Donors can also do much more to build awareness about the benefits of renewable energy in Iraq. They should focus on supporting pilot renewable energy initiatives that can have an outsized influence on perceptions of energy. These could include installing solar panels on institutions that have high public visibility, such as universities and malls. They should then experiment with more creative ways to publicize success stories, including by producing television segments.

Donors should also practice what they preach by integrating renewable technology into their own operations. They should put greater emphasis on prioritizing renewable energy and energy efficiency in reconstruction efforts and install solar panels on their offices, whenever feasible.

Deploying more renewable technology would advance several donor priorities in Iraq, including stabilization, the return of displaced populations, economic development, and job creation. It would also serve the geopolitical aims of Western and Arab Gulf donors by helping to reduce Iran's influence in Iraq.

DYLAN COLLINS/AFP via Getty Images

LEBANON THE DELIBERATE COLLAPSE

When two of Lebanon's power stations overheated to dangerous levels in 2019, Yahya Mawloud knew something was amiss.

The Zouk and Jiyeh power plants were just two years old and should not have been facing any technical issues. Mawloud, the chief operating officer of the company that managed the stations, consulted a German expert who assessed that low-grade fuel was the only possible culprit. Mawloud submitted a complaint to Lebanon's Ministry of Energy and Water Resources (MEW), but the answer came back that the fuel had been inspected when it arrived at the port of Beirut and was up to standard. Mawloud was not convinced.

After issuing more than 70 complaints, he took matters into his own hands and sent fuel samples to a laboratory in Dubai. The results confirmed his suspicions. As much as 30 percent of the fuel for the power stations had been siphoned off and replaced with a low-grade substitute. The adulterated fuel was sold to the stations at full price, and the stolen fuel was sold on the black market. It was a multibillion-dollar swindle. A UN official in Beirut said that the only plausible explanation was that the company importing the fuel had been bribing the MEW and the Lebanese laboratories that conducted the tests.[84] A BBC Arabic investigation found links between the two primary businesses involved in the scheme and leaders across Lebanon's political and sectarian spectrum.[85]

Lebanon's "dirty fuel" scandal is just one manifestation of the long-standing and deep-rooted corruption and mismanagement that has brought Lebanon's electricity sector to the verge of collapse in recent years. Opportunists have banded together to profit at the expense of the public at every level of the electricity sector. The public utility now struggles to provide even two hours of service a day, and many areas of the country get no state power at all. Lebanon represents the failure of past donor interventions to support the foundations of good governance in the electricity sector and their inability to effect positive change after networks of graft take hold of electricity systems. The government resists calls from international donors for reform because it is against the political elite's interests to provide reliable and affordable energy. And even if political will to reform the sector emerged, the central government lacks the capacity to do so. It can no longer finance basic maintenance of the sector or embark on strategic initiatives, and its bureaucratic capacity has been crippled—most civil servants do not show up to work.

However, there is a faint silver lining to Lebanon's tragic collapse. The current crisis has limited some actors' ability to profit, weakened

Major Electricity Infrastructure in Lebanon

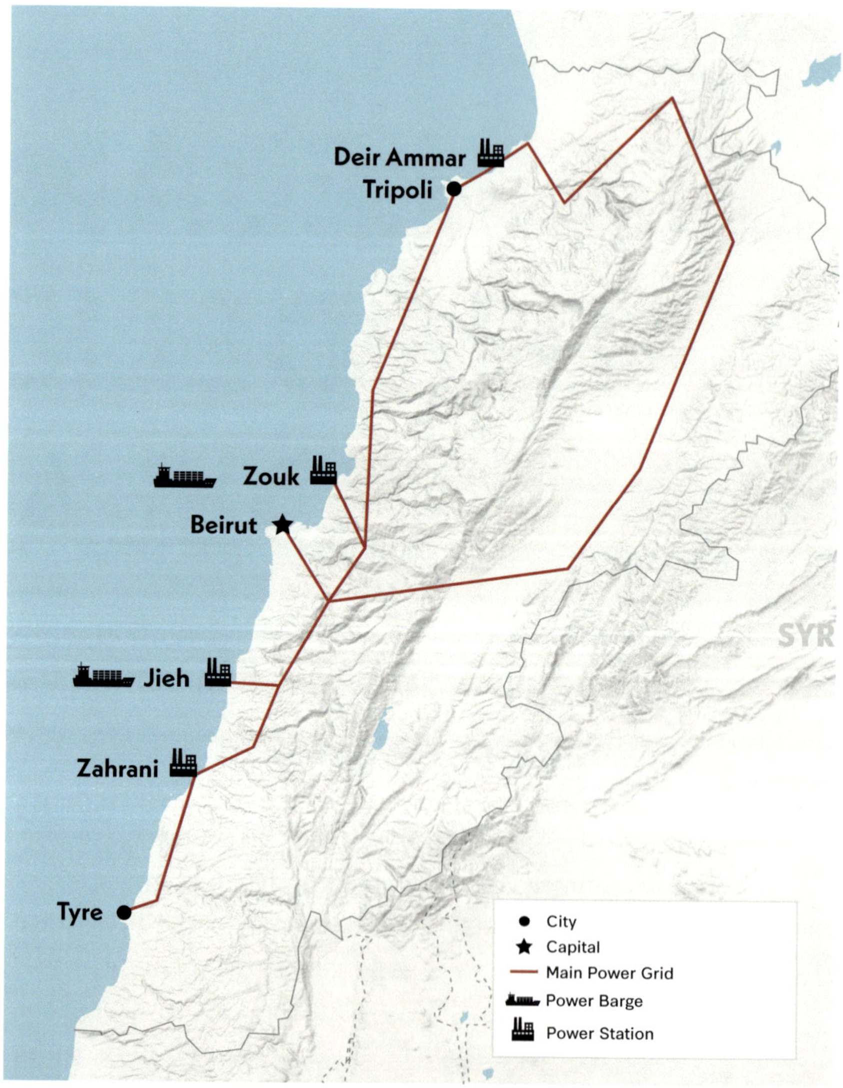

Source: Adapted from Waylon Fairbanks, "Lebanon's New Energy Minister Talks to MEES," MEES, June 14, 2019, https://www.mees.com/2019/6/14/power-water/lebanons-new-energy-minister-talks-to-mees/44cba470-8ea4-11e9-8a53-4706c33b6e44.

vested interests, and created new openings to reimagine the system. The crisis has forced the government to lift energy subsidies, and renewable technologies are now the most cost-effective solution for many Lebanese. Donors cannot work effectively with the central government because of its lack of capacity, and they will not be able to circumvent all grifters in the electricity sector. However, if they provide the right incentives to the right people to transition to renewables at a community-level, they can help plant the seeds of a quiet revolution in the electricity sector.

RECONSTRUCTION

Lebanon's post-war reconstruction process cemented clientelism and dysfunction in the electricity sector. The civil war destroyed much of Lebanon's electricity infrastructure, and Israel's 2006 war on Lebanon further downgraded it.[86] As former sectarian warlords transitioned into political leaders in the post-war period, the weakness of the electricity sector allowed them to shape both the formal and informal provision of electricity. Sectarian leaders secured kickbacks from large electricity infrastructure construction projects and simultaneously formed close ties with private generator owners, who supplemented the still inadequate state services and charged high tariffs.

> "The current crisis has limited some actors' ability to profit, weakened vested interests, and created new openings to reimagine the system.

The reconstruction process embedded deep inequalities in electricity provision and created opportunities for graft. Electricity reconstruction prioritized Beirut at the expense of Lebanon's peripheries, which have since endured much longer daily power outages than the capital. The government spent an estimated $3.66 billion on electricity sector projects from 1990 to 2019, yet it did so with limited oversight.[87] For example, it has failed to establish an independent regulator for the electricity sector in the last two decades, despite a 2002 law that mandated the creation of one.[88] The government focused on rebuilding the national utility, Electricité du Liban (EDL), while excluding alternative large-scale power providers. EDL's monopoly on the generation, transmission, and distribution of electricity strangled competition, created an important vulnerability, and exacerbated opportunities for corruption. EDL still controls more than 90 percent of the electricity sector and has not been subject to regular independent audits.[89]

International donors provided substantial reconstruction funding without establishing the foundations of good governance. They contributed $1.28 billion in funding for electricity projects through Lebanon's Council for Development and Reconstruction from 1992 to 2021, of which $1.24 billion was spent on rehabilitation and construction and just $38 million was spent on efforts to improve governance.[90] This assistance was funneled through the state and its affiliated networks of patronage and clientelism.[91]

Political actors came to see Lebanon's dysfunctional electricity sector as both a business and a political tool. High levels of state spending provided several opportunities for political actors to exploit. Government spending in the electricity sector from 1992 to 2019, including subsidies, accounted for an estimated $40 billion, equivalent to 40 percent of Lebanon's government debt.[92] One of the greatest areas of graft is in the import of fuel for power stations, which entails opaque contracting processes and large commissions for a tight-knit cartel.[93] The "dirty fuel" scandal is believed to be the tip of the iceberg—the Lebanese state has spent more than $24 billion on fuel imports to operate power plants since 1992.[94]

Temporary solutions to increase electricity generation have become additional avenues for money making. In 2013, the MEW signed a deal with a Turkish company to purchase energy from two power barges moored off the coast of Lebanon. The idea was to compensate for a reduction in capacity while old power plants were renovated and to save money on land licensing. The deal would have been sensible if it had been temporary, but it was not. The government renewed the contracts in 2016 and 2018 for a total sum of $1.5 billion, excluding the cost of fuel, which the government provided separately. The amount spent on the rental contracts is greater than the cost of purchasing the barges outright. Investigations revealed an alleged commission of $6 million for intermediaries, suspiciously poor negotiating by the Lebanese government, and opaque tendering processes.[95]

Private generators have also become a symbol of graft in Lebanon. In 2018, the World Bank estimated that more than a million people in Lebanon relied on subscriptions to 32,000 commercial generators, which represented a $1.1 billion annual market.[96] Neighborhood "generator mafias" have become a formidable political power, often enjoying close relationships with local and national political leaders. In addition to

Solar panels in the industrial zone by Zouk power plant.

JOSEPH EID/AFP via Getty Images

charging high prices for their services and enjoying local monopolies, generator owners developed economic interests in the dysfunctional status quo. They have worked to frustrate initiatives that would improve state electricity provision and undercut their profits. When the government rented a third Turkish barge in 2017 and needed to identify a location for it to unload its power, generator owners organized protests and sit-ins to prevent the power from being delivered to their areas.[97]

Unequal electricity provision and uncollected payments serve political goals. EDL not only has high technical losses, but it also operates with significant nontechnical losses, including illegal connections, falsified electricity meters, and uncollected bills.[98] A Lebanese electricity sector official said, "Politicians exempt certain regions from paying bills and collude with EDL to prioritize electricity provision to their constituencies."[99] For example, to boost popularity, members of parliament secure improved electricity for their hometowns before elections and when they visit.[100]

Despite the magnitude of problems in the electricity sector and its huge drain on state finances, no Lebanese government has embarked on a serious reform effort for the sector. Successive Lebanese governments have failed to establish an independent regulator for the electricity sector.

Donors began to appreciate the power of vested interests in the mid-2010s. The French government had provided tens of millions of dollars in technical assistance to EDL, and the World Bank proposed strategies to restructure the electricity sector. Still, change was scarce. In 2016, the World Bank's six-year country partnership framework assessed that the "absence of reform appetite" in the electricity sector meant it would not "plan significant financing programs at this time," despite reforms in the sector being "critical for the country to rise to the next level of development."[101] Donors had hoped that dangling the prospect of billions of dollars in soft loans at the 2018 CEDRE conference would incentivize reforms. It did not.[102] Arab Gulf states disengaged from Lebanon during the late 2010s due to the deteriorating security situation, Iran's growing influence, and their pessimism about the prospect of positive change.

THE RISE AND FALL OF THE BRIDE OF THE BEQAA

The "Bride of the Beqaa" captures the imagination of many Lebanese. The mountain city of Zahle overlooking the Beqaa plateau is famed for its beauty, pleasant climate, and quality arak. But for many years, Zahle was also famous for having 24/7 electricity without relying on neighborhood generators.

Electricité de Zahlé (EDZ) was established during the Ottoman era as a concession and maintained its status after EDL was created in 1964. Its electricity infrastructure was damaged in the civil war and subsequent Israeli attacks, and like the rest of Lebanon, private neighborhood generators spread to compensate for poor service. In 2014, EDZ leveraged its historic concession status to justify adopting a new approach. It contracted a British company to build a 35 MW power station, which supplied power during EDL outages.

EDZ embarked on a multipronged campaign to build support for its model and dislodge political opposition. It seized on Zahlawis' willingness to pay for better electricity by charging a rate in between the EDL rate and what they paid for private generators. These tariffs were profitable for EDZ while providing a more consistent and cheaper service for the public. EDZ also worked to build local support for its model. It provided patronage to NGOs, schools, churches, and journalists in exchange for support. It also conducted innovative marketing campaigns that linked pride in local identity with more reliable electricity. EDZ bought out some generator cartels and incorporated others into the new system by hiring them as employees. In conjunction with its local efforts, the company conducted long-term lobbying campaigns to build coalitions of support among the national elite.

However, EDZ's model suffered from several fatal flaws which the current crisis has laid bare. It relied on subsidized fuel and receiving EDL electricity at a discounted rate. When Lebanon's crisis hit, fuel prices soared and EDL services reduced, undercutting the basis of EDZ's business model. In August 2021, total blackouts returned to Zahle.

Had EDZ invested in renewable energy rather than relying on expensive fuel, it could have survived the collapse of the electricity sector and maintained its status as the bride of the Beqaa. Still, EDZ provides helpful lessons for circumventing political obstacles and producing local success stories.

Source: Adapted from Ali Ahmad et al., "From dysfunctional to functional corruption: the politics of decentralized electricity provision in Lebanon," *Energy Research & Social Science* 86 (April 2022), doi:10.1016/j.erss.2021.102399.

THE CURRENT CRISIS

Beginning in 2019, Lebanon's cascading crises caused an unprecedented collapse in the electricity sector. Dwindling foreign currency reserves rendered the government unable to finance fuel imports for electricity generation; the Beirut port explosion destroyed EDL's headquarters and key electricity infrastructure in Beirut; and both the government and EDL lost human capital in the accelerating brain drain, leaving them unable to maintain the grid or implement reforms. These crises have further diminished the government's capacity to shape the sector, but networks of corruption remain stubborn.

The collapse has had devastating impacts on consumers. Electricity production plummeted after EDL took several power stations offline, and areas of Lebanon have gone without state power for weeks at a time. Government electricity has also become more expensive because the government lifted fuel subsidies in 2021 and then raised electricity tariffs in November 2022.[103] Lebanese have been forced to resort to neighborhood generators for most of their electricity needs. Whereas private generators provided around 30 percent of electricity consumed in Lebanon prior to the crisis, they now provide more than 60 percent.[104] But these private supplies of electricity have become prohibitively expensive as well. A resident of the Bekaa valley said, "The amount of power I need to keep lights on and charge a mobile phone costs a government employee's monthly salary," while the owner of a trendy Beirut café said his monthly electricity bill had increased from $200 to $4,000.[105]

Rather than working to improve the governance of the electricity sector, Lebanese leaders have pursued short-term strategies to obtain more fuel. The government signed a deal with Iraq to exchange medical services for heavy fuel in 2021 and renewed the deal in 2022.[106] In August 2021, Hezbollah announced that it had forged an agreement to import fuel from Iran, in defiance of U.S. sanctions. Just hours later, the U.S. ambassador to Lebanon announced deals to import gas from Egypt and electricity from Jordan with World Bank financing.[107] If implemented, these World Bank deals would provide short-term relief, but they would add to Lebanon's debt. Even so, these deals remain in limbo at the time of writing, as they are conditional on reforms that the government has yet to complete.

Lebanese politicians are using the prospect of future domestic gas production in Lebanon as a justification for delaying reforms. In October 2022, Israel and Lebanon agreed to demarcate their maritime border in a U.S.-brokered deal, which opens the door to commercial gas exploration in Lebanese waters. However, gas reserves have not been proven, and even if they exist, they may take years to exploit. Lebanon will likely have to export most of the gas in order to attract investment, meaning little of it could be used domestically to produce electricity.

Despite Lebanon's renewable energy potential and the difficulty in securing fuel, the government has made little progress in implementing large-scale renewable projects. For example, Lebanon still has no utility-scale solar or wind projects.[108] When the MEW presented a plan for the electricity sector to donors in February 2022, it focused overwhelmingly on hydrocarbon generation

"

Rather than working to improve the governance of the electricity sector, Lebanese leaders have pursued short-term strategies to obtain more fuel.

rather than renewables.[109] The most promising initiative is the draft Distributed Renewable Energy (DRE) law, which the cabinet approved in April 2022. The law would be a catalyst for investment, break EDL's monopoly, and allow private individuals to sell electricity. However, it has not passed parliament at the time of writing, and Lebanese energy analysts fear that parliamentarians will amend it to reduce its impact and ensure that their allies can continue to profit in the electricity sector.[110]

The unwillingness of the political elite to implement any serious reforms, despite the unprecedented electricity crisis, prompted a UN official to say that interests that favor dysfunction are "a bigger monster than donors want to admit."[111] But even if the political elite finally accepted the necessity of reform, they do not have the capacity to implement them. Lebanon is facing multiple crises concurrently, and the government does not have sufficient political capital to address the electricity sector.

Further, the country struggles with a lack of human capacity. A Ministry of Finance official estimated that 6 in 10 state employees are either leaving or planning to leave Lebanon, a rate not seen since the civil war.[112] One EDL employee, working from a prefab building next to the remains of the headquarters, said that he is the only member of his original four-person team who still shows up to work.[113] The loss of human capital means that state institutions will struggle to implement reforms. As one UN official put it: "If the DRE law passed, EDL would likely receive thousands of applications for net metering. They could not even attempt to process those applications."[114]

OPPORTUNITIES FOR RENEWABLES

While vested interests remain stubborn at the central level, Lebanon's crisis has created more space for adaptations at the local level. Many Lebanese households have turned to renewables to compensate for the lack of state electricity. Starting from almost no installed renewable capacity in 2010, the market for domestic solar systems grew to 100 MW by 2019.[115] The current crisis prompted an exponential growth in solar, and the total installed capacity doubled to 200 MW in 2021 and is estimated to have doubled again to 400 MW by the end of 2022.[116] Most Lebanese who can afford domestic-level systems have now bought them, and they are a common sight on rooftops across the country.

However, domestic solar systems are not a comprehensive solution to Lebanon's electricity crisis. Eighty-five percent of Lebanese now live below the poverty line, and without access to financing, renewable technology remains out of reach for Lebanon's poorest households. In some cases, families have sold their family jewelry to be able to afford solar technology for their house, and many are now unable to afford maintenance.[117] Lebanon's financial crisis has ended most low-interest loans for solar technology, meaning those without substantial savings cannot purchase domestic systems.[118] Only al-Qard al-Hassan, a Hezbollah-affiliated organization that appears to retain its own foreign currency reserves, gives loans to customers in U.S. dollars.[119] However, loans that require repayment in dollars are risky for most customers whose salaries are paid in Lebanese lira, as the lira continues to devaluate against the dollar. The Housing Bank launched a program to provide loans for solar technology in Lebanese lira, but the potential for further devaluation makes it a risky investment for the bank, as it may not be able to recuperate the full value of its loans.[120] Those risks deter independent power purchasing agreements and investments in peer-to-peer systems as well.

The government opted not to regulate the solar market in order to facilitate its growth, but the lack of regulation prompted a flood of poor-quality and second-hand technology. Government officials have warned of a coming backlash against renewable energy when many of these systems inevitably start to break in coming months and years. The Lebanese Center for Energy Conservation has begun to publish a list of qualified solar companies that can participate in the Housing Bank scheme, but a lack of awareness about high-quality products continues to undermine the market.[121] With no process for the safe disposal of solar equipment or batteries, faulty technology will also create environmental hazards.[122]

At least 17 communities across Lebanon have adopted hybrid mini-grids that combine solar panels and diesel generators to compensate for the weakness of the central grid.[123] These neighborhood systems follow different business models. Some are implemented by municipalities, some are private enterprises, and others are community-owned initiatives, but they all share several common features. Most seek to integrate solar power into preexisting neighborhood generator grids, reduce the reliance on diesel, and provide consumers with cheaper and more reliable energy.[124]

Although small in scale, each of these initiatives have had to overcome different political and economic interests. Some still risk sabotage by the political elite, which fears losing its monopoly. EDL is currently suing one private project in Jabbouleh, arguing that the project depends on the illegal use of some state infrastructure.[125] Powerful economic interests exist at the local level as well. As the director of the Lebanese Foundation for Renewable Energy noted, when seeking to integrate solar panels into local electricity networks, "Municipalities that own their own generators are low-hanging fruit." Those projects do not compete with private generator owners, who are often hostile to initiatives that break their monopolies or undercut their business.[126] However, some projects have successfully collaborated with or coopted generator owners. Because fuel prices have increased to the extent that some customers can no longer afford their services, the crisis has made some generator owners more open to change. It is in their interest to adopt a new system that still provides them with some profits. The crisis has therefore weakened the generator mafia and opened more space for experimentation with new systems of electricity provision.

BAALOUL VERDE

Baaloul is not like most towns in Lebanon. Perched on the side of a mountain in the Bekaa Valley, Baaloul's Sunni-majority inhabitants do not use any of Lebanon's three most common languages—Arabic, English, and French. Instead, the lingua franca is Spanish. Many residents of Baaloul migrated to Latin America during the civil war and then returned to rebuild their homes after its end. The ties between South America and the small town remain and contribute to residents' strong sense of local identity.

But hearing Spanish on the streets is not the only striking thing about Baaloul. It also has reliable electricity.

In 2012, the residents of Baaloul endured up to 12 hours of power cuts from the state a day and relied on dirty individual generators or expensive private ones. They came together as a community to find a solution. The collective raised $300,000 in donations from their members and relatives in South America and invested in their own diesel-powered mini-grid. The residents of the town own the mini-grid, manage it collectively, set tariffs, and share the profits. Installing their own system reduced electricity bills by 50 percent.

In 2018, Baaloul received $200,000 from USAID to hybridize the mini-grid by installing solar panels, on the condition that they provide power to Syrian refugees living nearby. With reduced diesel consumption, profit margins increased, and electricity bills were cut in half again.

After Lebanon's 2019 crisis, residents report that the state stopped providing any electricity at all, but the community's grid cushioned the blow. Today, Baaloul's grid provides 13 hours of power a day, and although the cost of diesel has gone up, solar energy continues to offset costs.

Baaloul demonstrates the potential for communities to create their own solutions to dire economic problems, capitalize on local solidarity, and then enhance their system with additional donor funding.

Source: Author's remote interviews with residents of Baaloul, October 27, 2022; and Alix Chaplain, "Strategies of power and the emergence of hybrid mini-grids in Lebanon," Jadaliyya, March 8, 2022, https://www.jadaliyya.com/Details/43932.

DONOR STRATEGIES

The complexity of the political, economic, and financial crisis has caused a breakdown in donor unity on the best way to support Lebanon's electricity sector. Donors have grown increasingly critical of the Lebanese elite in public. Senior UN officials have described Lebanon as a "failing state," and the World Bank has described Lebanon's collapse as "deliberate."[127]

However, one group of donors, which includes the World Bank, the International Monetary Fund (IMF), and Japan, continues to believe that state-level reforms are the only way to solve Lebanon's electricity crisis and insists on working through the government. This group is pushing the government to unbundle the electricity sector, continue to reform subsidies, and establish the Electricity Regulatory Authority (ERA).

Other donors do not see any serious appetite for reform. An official from a European donor noted, "Lebanese officials continue to complain about our reform demands and think they can convince us to just give them cash instead."[128] They fear that the government may implement fig-leaf reforms that preserve the elite's ability to block accountability. For example, Western donors believe the government could implement a version of the ERA that the elite can hamstring. A UN official warned, "If they have an even number of seats on the board of the regulator which are appointed by sectarian parties, gridlock will continue."[129]

Therefore, a second group of donors, which includes the United States, France, and some UN agencies, has determined that their interventions are most effective when implemented with limited state involvement.[130] France is pushing the aid response to the Beirut blast to work with governorates and municipalities instead of the central state.[131] Several UN agencies have found that they are most effective when working directly with individual institutions. They work to support the resilience of critical infrastructure such as hospitals, water pumping stations, and schools by installing renewables as a backup electricity source.[132]

This group of donors is supporting various local renewable projects across Lebanon. USAID's $29 million INARA project is the most promising and largest-scale example, as it seeks to reach 50,000 beneficiaries.[133] The project began with a legal analysis to identify sustainable renewable energy interventions in the current environment. Despite the restrictive legal context, they determined that several types of intervention at the local level are feasible within the current legal framework.[134] INARA is working to rehabilitate hydropower infrastructure and install solar systems to clusters of municipalities and individual homes. In July 2022, USAID hosted a launch event to rehabilitate the hydroelectric plant at Rechmaya, which will improve electricity provision for 23,000 people in 17 nearby communities that only receive two hours of electricity a day.[135] USAID also put out a call for applications from clusters of municipalities that could host its first solar intervention, a utility-scale power plant of up to 7 MW which aims to cover a third of electricity usage for 30,000 beneficiaries.[136]

Although the project appears to be pursuing several promising interventions, it has been shrouded in secrecy, and other donors that are seeking to support Lebanon's electricity infrastructure complain that opportunities to collaborate, share best practices, and expand the scale of the project are being squandered.[137] Some energy experts suggested that USAID is not collaborating with other donors for political reasons. One analyst argued, "The United States wants to be able to point to the impact of a project solely implemented by USAID to counter accusations from Hezbollah and others that U.S. policy is causing suffering in Lebanon." However, members of the INARA team assert that they plan to collaborate with other donors and attract other sources of funding once they have demonstrated success stories that can be replicated.[138]

"

Donors will not bring about transformative change in Lebanon's electricity sector by supporting local projects unless they can facilitate access to more significant sources of financing.

The UN Economic and Social Commission for Western Asia has also implemented pilot projects that aim to demonstrate how renewable technology can provide broader development benefits. These projects have supported women's cooperatives and include capacity building on how to generate income, reduce inefficiencies, and increase revenues to show that renewable energy technology can enable economic development and advance gender equity.[139]

However, donors will not bring about transformative change in Lebanon's electricity sector by supporting local projects unless they can facilitate access to more significant sources of financing. Even the target beneficiaries of USAID's ambitious INARA project represent less than 1 percent of Lebanon's population. Some sources of alternative financing, such as development bonds, climate financing, and corporate social responsibility funds, have been underutilized in Lebanon and could provide opportunities to scale up. Development impact bonds are attractive to donors because they facilitate private sector-led experimentation in the local context and public actors only pay for projects that have successful social outcomes. Investors also benefit as they get a financial and social return on their investment.[140] Similarly, many climate funds have little uptake but provide important funding for renewable technologies.[141] And overseas companies could be convinced to invest in Lebanon's green transition as a form of corporate social responsibility, particularly if they employ members of the Lebanese diaspora.[142]

CONCLUSION: WEAK CENTRAL CAPACITY AND ENTRENCHED INTERESTS IN THE STATUS QUO

When Lebanon entered its reconstruction phase in the 1990s, renewables were not a viable option for the electricity sector. Because reconstruction efforts have led to the development of cronyism and corruption, it is very difficult to transform the sector. Donors have tried to dangle aid to incentivize reforms in Lebanon's electricity sector for over 30 years. This strategy failed to avert the current electricity crisis because the political elite have developed deep interests in the dysfunctional status quo and have colluded to protect it. Even Lebanon's unprecedented collapse over the past three years has not prompted the government to implement the necessary reforms to set the electricity sector on a path to recovery. The government has not unbundled EDL nor enacted a legal framework for distributed renewable energy, and it has only just taken the first steps to establish an independent electricity regulator.[143]

Lebanon's current crises have severely limited the central government's capacity, which undermines its ability to implement reforms. In these conditions, most donors have rightly concluded that there is little utility in attempting to work with the central government to fix Lebanon's electricity sector. They should continue to insist on reforms as a precondition for major financial assistance and should be wary of short-term solutions that add to Lebanon's debt without opening any space for reform.

The cost of government inaction is rising as the situation continues to deteriorate. Donors are right to implement emergency humanitarian projects to support the resilience of critical infrastructure, but they should also expand their efforts to support community-level renewable energy projects and scale them up by unlocking sources of alternative financing. These projects require shifts in donor approaches and a nuanced understanding of the local political economy to avoid spoilers. However, there are examples of success and alternatives are possible.

Community-based projects will bring benefits that extend far beyond the electricity sector. They can contribute to Lebanon's green transition, serve as the foundation for local economic development, and show Lebanese that there is an alternative to the corrupt political elite.

MAHMUD TURKIA/AFP via Getty Images

LIBYA A CRISIS OF MANAGEMENT, NOT RESOURCES

In Libya's capital city, Tripoli, Mahmud sleeps in the back of his car with his two toddlers. The 48-year-old pulls the back seats down and lays out blankets. "This is my bedroom," he says. Mahmud is not displaced or homeless. In fact, his car is parked in his garage.

He is forced to share this tiny space with his family to escape the sweltering Libyan summers, finding relief in the confines of his air-conditioned car.[144] The combination of Libya's heavy fuel subsidies and its dysfunctional electricity sector make it more affordable for Mahmud to sleep in his car with the engine running than purchase a private generator to cool his house. Mahmud's story is similar to millions of Libyans who suffer long power cuts and are unable to afford alternative supplies of electricity.

Libya's electricity sector has deteriorated markedly since Muammar al-Gaddafi was forced from power in 2011. In 2020, the electricity crisis peaked when the General Electricity Company of Libya (GECOL) was only able to generate 3,800 MW during the summer, well short of the 7,500 MW load needed.[145] Rolling blackouts became a staple of hot summers in the country, and power outages averaged 14 to 18 hours a day. Power cuts affected not only households but also hospitals, schools, communications networks, water pumping stations, and industries. They brought life to a halt in the country, worsened living conditions, and raised social tensions.

Although Libya has significant potential for renewable energy, much like Iraq, various aspects of the political economy and ongoing instability undermine its feasibility. Over decades, Libyans have come to expect cheap electricity from the government, and that deters the government from attempting the necessary subsidy reform that would make alternative forms of electricity provision competitive. GECOL's monopoly over the electricity sector and the interests that other Libyan state actors have in the status quo also stymie efforts to diversify the energy mix.

Rehabilitating the electricity sector in Libya is proving to be a painful undertaking for the government and the donor community alike. Together, the legacy of a failed socialist system, corruption, and networks of patronage constrain reform efforts. Following a decade of stabilization projects, donors believe a major overhaul of the grid and GECOL's operations is needed.[146] Plans include unbundling GECOL, bringing utility-scale renewable energy technology into the mix, and making renewables an attractive option for state actors and end consumers.[147]

Yet, three main obstacles undermine donor efforts for development of the electricity

Major Energy Infrastructure and Zones of Control in Libya

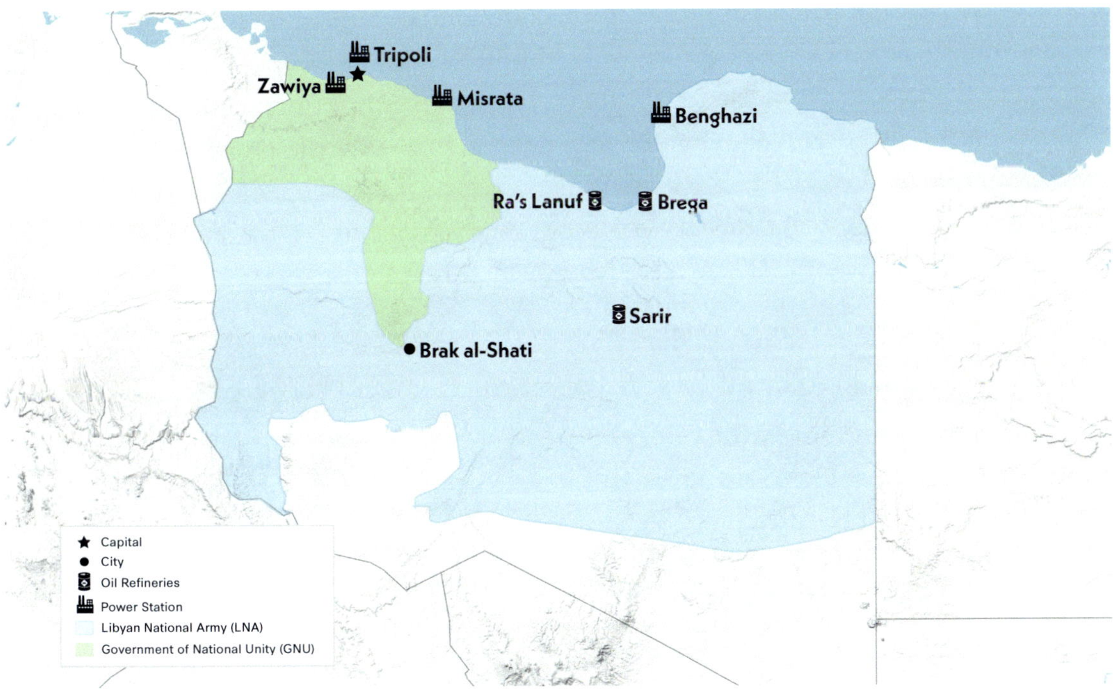

Source: Adapted from Alia Chughtai and Ramy Allahoum, "Libya: Mapping areas of military control," Aljazeera, July 27, 2020, https://www.aljazeera.com/news/2020/7/27/libya-mapping-areas-of-military-control; and Mohamed Almaktar, A.M. Elbreki, and Mohamed Shaaban, "Revitalizing operational reliability of the electrical energy system in Libya: Feasible analysis of solar generation in local communities," *Journal of Cleaner Production* 279 (January 2021): 123647, https://doi.org/10.1016/j.jclepro.2020.123647.

sector. The first is political instability. The fluid, transitional nature of governments since 2011 has been a constant obstacle. Political actors rotate in and out of power, erasing institutional memory and previously established partnerships with international donors. The second obstacle is the country's political economy. Subsidies have been a durable barrier to attracting investment in alternatives and have encouraged unsustainable energy consumption. The last obstacle is hydrocarbon wealth and the oil industry's strong influence on financing and production in the electricity sector, which has allowed the government to keep a failing national electricity system afloat.

PRIOR WEAKNESS

Prior to 2011, Libya's oil wealth allowed the government to provide cheap and relatively reliable electricity for decades, obfuscating the sector's weaknesses. The Gaddafi regime established GECOL in the 1980s as a vertically integrated, state-owned utility company. One of two electricity sector monopolies left in Africa, GECOL now controls every aspect of the value chain, from generation and transmission to distribution and sales.[148] While GECOL's poor management has led to structural and operational weaknesses, the company continues to hold sole control over the market. Heavy energy subsidies and the absence of an energy regulatory framework make competition futile. Private sector actors struggle for return on investment when competing with an electricity price of $0.004 per kilowatt-hour (kWh), which is about 5 percent of the prevailing cost in the Washington, D.C., region and one of the lowest costs in the world.[149] Under Gaddafi, the state was in full control.

Gaddafi made little effort to diversify state electricity production. The government tentatively began to explore renewable energy, and it created the Renewable Energy Agency of Libya (REAoL) in 2007. However, the agency did very little, and oil and gas continued to dominate international involvement in the energy sector. As a result, the sector was vulnerable to shocks in global oil markets and disruptions in domestic production.

While the sector bled cash, that did not pose a problem for the Gaddafi government, which had adopted energy subsidies as a mode of wealth distribution in exchange for the public's political acquiescence. It coupled low electricity tariffs with widespread electrification, and the strategy set the stage for a culture of wasteful power consumption.[150] Consumers viewed plentiful electricity as their cut of the country's oil wealth, and Libyan consumption surpassed Tunisia's, which has twice the population.[151]

THE CURRENT CRISIS

Libya's post-revolution turmoil laid bare the deep issues in its electricity sector. Whereas electricity provision in Libya depends on a healthy nexus of central financial management and oil and gas production to keep its operations running, more than a decade of armed conflict and political instability has undermined both.

Oil is Libya's greatest prize, and conflict for it has thrown electricity production into disarray. The National Oil Corporation (NOC)—a state-owned entity—controls oil production, pricing, and sales and transfers profits to the Central Bank of Libya (CBL). In turn, the CBL funds the government's budget and finances spending on utilities and public salaries.[152] Since 2014, rival governments have emerged in eastern and western Libya.[153] The UN-backed Government of National Unity (GNU), based in western Libya and led by Prime Minister Dbeibah, is locked in conflict with the parliament in the east, which is supported by Khalifa Haftar's Libyan National Army (LNA). Each has sought to exert control over the NOC, CBL, and GECOL. Fighting between the two sides—and the security forces loyal to them—has interrupted oil production and undermined electricity provision, exacerbating GECOL's mounting operational challenges.[154] And the problems are intertwined. Not only do the electrical generation facilities require oil and gas to fuel them, but oil and gas production itself requires electricity. In 2020, Khalifa Haftar enforced a blockade on key oil refineries in the east, costing the state $11 billion in revenues and worsening electricity and fuel shortages throughout the country.[155]

In addition, deteriorating security left the grid vulnerable to vandalism and theft, pushed foreign contractors and engineers to leave, and drove out foreign direct investment.[156] The loss of human capital hurt GECOL's ability to perform regular maintenance work and jeopardized the operating capacity of several control rooms, generation units, and transmission lines.[157]

Corruption has also weakened the electricity sector since the revolution, with transparency becoming a key issue. Following an in-depth review of the company's dealings, the Libyan Audit Bureau (LAB) accused GECOL of corrupt contracting processes and criticized the slow execution of several projects, many of which have remained in the pipeline years after their target completion dates.[158] Working to introduce more accountability for GECOL and its top management, the LAB referred their investigation results to Libya's attorney general and recommended a travel ban on senior GECOL officials in 2020.[159] Several probes into GECOL's managerial conduct followed. As a result of those investigations, the LAB threatened to rescind contracts approved for GE, Siemens, and Turkish contractor Çalık Enerji and award them to other companies unless GECOL provided more transparency into the causes of delays.[160] These companies are heavyweight foreign partners

> **"Not only do the electrical generation facilities require oil and gas to fuel them, but oil and gas production itself requires electricity.**

for GECOL and often win multimillion-dollar contracts for equipment and maintenance, dominating the state-sponsored electricity sector projects.[161]

Meanwhile, service quality plummeted. In 2020, severe technical issues and poor maintenance of equipment forced GECOL to implement rolling blackouts as it failed to meet demand.[162] Electricity shortages are acute in densely populated, highly electrified urban centers, areas where consumption continues to increase, most noticeably over the summer.[163] Electricity subsidies continue to represent a heavy financial burden for the state. They crowd major private actors out of the market and disincentivize energy efficiency.[164] In 2019 alone, gasoline and electricity accounted for close to 70 percent of Libya's $5.4 billion subsidy budget.[165] The underpricing of electricity and GECOL's weak fee-collection mechanisms encourage a sense of entitlement to state energy, increasing Libyans' unsustainable consumption. According to a recent LAB report, GECOL failed to collect bills worth over $900 million from end consumers in 2021.[166] Despite the heavy financial burden, a lack of political will prevents the government from implementing subsidy reform. Cheap state electricity remains a core pillar of the legitimacy of these competing authorities. Reforming subsidy policies without improving electricity provision would result in public backlash.

With households, schools, and hospitals left without state power, Libyans began to seek off-grid alternatives. Libyans are increasingly turning to private electricity providers at the domestic level, indicating that they are prepared to pay for electricity, just not from the state, leading to the emergence of a market for private generators. Local businesses import Italian, Chinese, and Turkish equipment and use social media to connect with customers. Individuals and businesses offer generators and maintenance services for sale over Facebook groups, one of which has gained over 50,000 members in recent years.[167] Operating costs are relatively low, as generators can take advantage of subsidized fuel.[168] However, private generators require an initial investment of $500 to $5,000, which is unaffordable for many.[169]

A Libyan repairman, assisted by sub-Saharan African workers, tries to start a generator at a workshop in Tripoli.

MAHMUD TURKIA/AFP via Getty Images

Amid the country's electricity crisis, Libyans came together at the local neighborhood level. Research for this study shows that generators have built community solidarity, with some Libyans sharing their privately generated electricity with neighbors who cannot afford to purchase a generator themselves. In the summer of 2022, a photo of Haitham Al-Ghoul, a Benghazi resident, went viral on social media. Haitham was holding his five-year-old son Othman, whose respirator was hooked to a private generator offered by a shop in their neighborhood.[170] Fuel subsidies make producing electricity relatively cheap for the individual. However, subsidies are also a key obstacle to Libya's ability to capitalize on its potential for renewables.

BLAME IT ON THE BITCOIN

Libyans struggled to keep cool during the summer of 2022, with rolling blackouts that lasted up to 18 hours a day. As public outrage mounted, Libya's internationally recognized prime minister, Abdul Hamid Dbeibah, found a new culprit for the country's power woes: "secret" bitcoin mining operations he says are popping up across the country.

The popularity of bitcoin mining—officially illegal in Libya—has skyrocketed in recent years. In 2021, Libyans reportedly mined about 0.6 percent of all of the bitcoin in the world. That put Libya ahead of every country in the Arab world and Africa, and ahead of every European country but Norway, courtesy of Libya's low cost of electricity.

Bitcoin mining uses high-power computers to solve complex math problems in exchange for payment in newly minted bitcoins. The requisite computational power sucks up a lot of energy. Mining a single bitcoin can use as much electricity as a typical U.S. household uses in nine years. Libya prices a kilowatt-hour (kWh) of electricity as low as $0.004—this equates to roughly 1/40th of the U.S. average of $0.16 per kWh and about 1/16th the price in China, the world's leading miner of bitcoins. And many Libyans do not even pay their electrical bills due to lax enforcement.

The government blames bitcoin miners for the country's poor electricity service. Globally, bitcoin mining consumes an estimated 97 terawatt-hours (TWh) of power a year—with Libya's portion accounting for 2 percent of the country's total output. Even so, the government says any increased demand has an outsized effect in a country already reeling from an electricity deficit.

Critics of the government point out that Libya's electricity problems long predate bitcoin mining. Libya's capacity to generate electricity has declined since 2013, and the country can only meet two-thirds of peak summer demand. Even without bitcoin miners, current capacity would still fall far short. Furthermore, the government may be part of the problem in other ways. Some analysts have traced bitcoin mining activity to buildings housing official government offices.

Source: Tabadul Channel, "مزارع تعدين البتكوين في ليبيا - الجزء الأول" [Bitcoin mining farms in Libya - Part one], YouTube video, September 7, 2021, https://www.youtube.com/watch?; "Country Analysis Executive Summary: Libya," U.S. Energy Information Administration, Last updated May 9, 2022, https://www.eia.gov/international/content/analysis/countries_long/Libya/pdf/libya.pdf; "Electricity prices," Global Petrol Prices.com, June 2022, https://www.globalpetrolprices.com/electricity_prices/; Jon Huang et al., "Bitcoin Uses More Electricity Than Many Countries. How Is That Possible?," *New York Times*, September 3, 2021, https://www.nytimes.com/interactive/2021/09/03/climate/bitcoin-carbon-footprint-electricity.html; The New Arab Staff, "Low-cost Libya becomes regional center for energy intensive bitcoin mining operations," New Arab, April 20, 2021, https://www.newarab.com/news/libya-becomes-regional-centre-bitcoin-mining-operation; "بعد حديث الدبيبة.. ما علاقة بيتكوين بأزمة الكهرباء في ليبيا؟" [After Dbeibeh's talk . . . What does bitcoin have to do with Libya's electricity crisis?], *Sky News Arabia*, July 11, 2022, http://bit.ly/3xncEz4; and Sami Zaptia, "Demonstrators block roads with makeshift fires in protest at lengthening power cuts," *Libya Herald*, June 30, 2022, https://www.libyaherald.com/2022/06/demonstrators-block-roads-with-makeshift-fires-in-protest-at-lengthening-power-cuts/.

OPPORTUNITIES FOR RENEWABLES

The scale of the electricity crisis has prompted some politicians to see diversification of the sector into renewables as a solution, but they have made little tangible progress. Both the Government of National Accord (GNA), in place from 2015 to 2021, and today's GNU integrated REAoL, the country's renewable energy agency created in 2007, into plans to diversify Libya's energy mix. In 2021, REAoL announced several solar renewable energy projects, one of which is projected to install around 2,000 MW through public-private partnership investments.[171] The GNU has also signed several other agreements with international companies, such as Total Energies, to build solar parks.[172] However, these plans have yet to materialize. Critics speculate that the GNU has pursued these projects merely to strengthen its ties with international actors and bolster its international claim to legitimacy.[173]

Despite Libyans' increasing receptivity to private electricity solutions, the capital costs of renewable energy technologies make them unaffordable for most Libyans. Muhammad Kowash, a development expert, said, "Powering an entire house using solar requires an investment of close to $16,000. This is outside citizens' financial means."[174] Even Libyans who could afford renewable technology have been hesitant to invest in it. Some view the electricity problems as a temporary issue that will somehow be solved, and others fear that equipment will be stolen or that there is insufficient technical expertise to maintain the systems. Still, some local communities and international donors have worked together to test renewable energy systems. These projects are small and ad hoc. In 2018, the UNDP began helping nine hospitals to install solar panels to support a more reliable and uninterrupted power supply for their operations.[175] While undoubtedly helpful for local communities, such initiatives exist in silos and are limited in terms of their scalability without a legal framework that opens the national grid for electricity produced privately from renewable energy sources. Libya would need to implement a net-metering scheme to provide a financial incentive for local initiatives to spread, as net contributors would be compensated for excess power pumped into the national grid.

Local and international development advisers emphasize the need to work with the central government on realistic solutions for the electricity crisis in Libya, including regulatory reform that improve energy efficiency requirements and open the doors to private sector investment, which can enable equitable access to electricity across the country.[176] Solutions must place reforming GECOL's operational style and tariff collection front and center but should also not preclude a role for international support for facilitating renewable energy options and linking them to the national grid.

DONOR STRATEGIES

International donors have limited ability to push for reform in Libya without parallel domestic political will. Initially donors adopted a light-touch approach toward Libya's political transition after the ouster of Gaddafi, providing support only when asked. Rather than immediate, insistent attempts to improve governance, donors prioritized peacebuilding projects, constitution building, elections, and stabilization through the disarmament, demobilization, and reintegration of armed groups.

Likewise, the electricity sector has proven especially resistant to change. Donors initially prioritized reform and rehabilitation through technical assistance, maintenance, and expert assessments. Though in time they also attempted to address operational issues and regulatory reform, but the Libyan government and GECOL were never able to push through with any changes.[177] However, without state-level commitment to reform—and without a government in the position to make such a commitment—technical interventions only served as life-support measures to keep the grid going.[178] Some donors have even argued that such interventions were counterproductive, creating the illusion that the national grid could be fixed, while other experts argue that it needs a complete overhaul.[179] Matthew Brubacher, an economic and energy adviser described Libya's electricity problems as endemic, due to two key issues. First, the electricity tariff charged to the consumer is far below market cost. Making matters worse, hardly any bills have been collected since 2011. This leads to wasteful consumption, which in turn has led to consumers using more than they need, doubling electricity consumption and denying GECOL of the necessary funds to invest in maintaining the electricity system. Second, GECOL continues to receive state subsidies regardless of its performance.[180]

However, donors continue to work with GECOL, as they see its neutrality as an important asset in an otherwise divided country. GECOL's physical grid links the two Libyan governments (the GNU in the west and Libya's parliament in the east) despite their political differences. Therefore, boosting GECOL's capacity could serve as a helpful step toward national reunification. USAID and their partners are ardent supporters of this approach and already work in partnership with GECOL and the CBL.[181] Economic development experts interviewed during this research believe that the solution is not only fixing equipment and generation units but also leveraging technical projects into development opportunities that can transform these systems completely, such as introducing renewables to the Libyan electricity grid to reduce supply issues.

However, donors cannot drive the transition to renewables in Libya. Successfully implementing and scaling solar projects requires long-term investment, but interest in renewables from international development agencies has come in waves.[182] Donor funding cycles and the short timeline on which stabilization missions operate mean that several key agencies tackling electricity are struggling to raise the necessary funds for even one-off solar projects. Additionally, Libya's shifting politics undermine the successful execution of projects. In June 2022, Prime Minister Dbeibah suspended the board of directors of GECOL, referred them to administrative investigation, and reinstated the board a week later with new leadership. Such turnover undermines institutional memory and donor relationships.[183]

While donors have little hope of transforming Libya's social contract, they can introduce some solutions to help address electricity-related grievances. For example, donors have had some success in supporting GECOL during episodes of frustration by municipalities over the loadshedding schedule back in 2018–2019. As the electricity situation continued to deteriorate, loadshedding became unavoidable to protect the grid from total shutdown. This resulted in several armed groups disabling the breakers to demonstrate that they could keep the lights on in their communities. This act of interference led to a complete shutdown of the grid. But with the support of partners like USAID and UNEP, GECOL and the ministry of local governance were able to identify that better communication about the loadshedding schedule can help show communities that it was done equitably. This effectively put an end to sabotage by armed groups. Once the municipalities and the larger electricity consumers, like the steel and cement companies, were on board with a common loadshedding schedule the situation improved and it was easier to make the repairs to restore the infrastructure.[184]

"

Donors continue to work with GECOL, as they see its neutrality as an important asset in an otherwise divided country. GECOL's physical grid links the two Libyan governments (the GNU in the west and Libya's parliament in the east) despite their political differences.

However, mounting public frustration with long power cuts is already putting Libya's rival governments and GECOL under pressure, creating a sense of urgency for quick, short-term fixes to electricity provision. This urgency is likely to impact the type of support the government requests from donors, pushing donors' long-term reform plans to the back in favor of quick stabilization of the grid. In 2022, protests broke out in Tripoli and Benghazi after rolling power cuts took a toll on civilians.[185] These protests were symptomatic of the public's view that the electricity crisis was caused by the government's poor performance and armed groups' interest in energy resources. State actors have blamed each other in an attempt to deflect public anger. Prime Minister Dbeibeh suspended GECOL's board of directors prior to the protests but still failed to keep public anger at bay.[186] The GNU also blamed Haftar's blockade of key oil fields in the east for impacting the public electricity grid.[187] GECOL then blamed the NOC for failing to provide gas to keep some of GECOL's stations online, with the NOC denying those accusations.[188]

With warring political factions fighting over energy resources, donors have limited ability to push for renewable energy in Libya. Their interventions are piecemeal and short term, and a range of vested interests thwart efforts at longer-term reform.

POLITICS AND VESTED INTERESTS

The Libyan electricity sector is often synonymous with GECOL, but there are many other actors in the field who resist reform. A small number of MNCs dominate the market. This group includes Siemens, GE, ENI, and Total Energies, with GE and Siemens winning the lion's share of most GECOL contracts.[189] Even GECOL's renewable energy projects are mostly done in cooperation with these companies. GECOL's favoritism was highlighted in 2020 when the LAB deemed a contract GECOL awarded to Siemens illegal because it was awarded through direct commission and Siemens had failed in the past to deliver a similar project.[190] Some local actors may even have an interest in ensuring large MNCs' monopoly over major government contracts where they can receive a handsome commission from brokering multimillion-dollar deals between GECOL and foreign contractors.[191] The dominance of MNCs crowds out private sector investment beyond GECOL and, subsequently, deters investment in renewable energy.

The government has also formed several joint ventures with MNCs and foreign states in the electricity sector. The public has limited awareness about the role of these entities in the sector, which gives them cover to pursue their interests quietly while letting GECOL absorb any political and social shocks related to their projects.[192] Since Libya's electrification, only two short-lived ministries have held responsibility for oversight of the electricity sector. The first ministry was established in 2007 and dissolved in 2009, and another—the Ministry of Electricity and Renewable Energy—was created in 2012 and dissolved in 2016. The 2012 decree that established the latter ministry outlined 12 bodies operating in the energy sector, making it one of the few sources that clearly names the companies that the state of Libya owns. Some are joint ventures between GECOL and MNCs such as Alstom and GE, while others are joint ventures between the Libyan state and foreign states such as Egypt, India, and Bulgaria.[193]

Such joint ventures give MNCs privileged access to the development and maintenance of the electricity sector in Libya at the expense

"

The Libyan electricity sector is often synonymous with GECOL, but there are many other actors in the field who resist reform.

of the local private sector, allowing these companies to enjoy some form of monopoly over contracts for equipment, maintenance, and even renewable energy projects.[194] It is not even clear if these companies still operate today. Even prior to the 2012 decree, few of these companies had a clear record of project implementation, and their published organizational charts lack any mention of members of their board of directors and general managers, further adding to issues of transparency in the electricity sector.

These different actors and their obscure influence in the electricity sector could complicate any push for reform that would jeopardize their exclusive access to lucrative electricity contracts.

CONCLUSION: STRONG CENTRAL CAPACITY AND ENTRENCHED INTERESTS IN THE STATUS QUO

To solve its electricity crisis, Libya needs subsidy reform, stronger institutions, and accountability mechanisms to prevent exploitation in the sector. Donors stand little chance of prompting these reforms in the current context as various actors have an interest in ongoing dysfunction in industries that affect electricity provision like oil and gas, or directly in the electricity sector itself. Prior to 2011, Libya had no need for donors, and most Libyan decisionmakers today remain distrustful of international donors and their intentions. This distrust complicates donor interventions in the electricity sector and limits opportunities for foreign investment in renewable energy. Unlike other conflict-affected states in this study, Libya does not need external funding, meaning efforts to leverage aid to encourage reform are unlikely to succeed. With stable oil production, Libya has the financial resources to recover from this crisis. It can cover its own government budget, including public salaries and operational costs for companies such as GECOL.

But the current lack of political will for major reforms does not shut the door to productive donor interventions on a smaller scale. Donors should seek opportunities to build trust with Libyan authorities by helping mediate communities' grievances associated with the electricity sector and leveraging these interventions to push for opportunities to integrate renewables. They could also better publicize the impact of their renewable energy projects to build public awareness and receptivity to alternative systems of electricity provision. Furthermore, donors can play a greater role in developing local capacities in the electricity sector.[195] As it stands, donors provide technical assistance and use foreign experts to conduct assessments. However, ongoing insecurity makes it progressively harder to keep foreign engineers in the country. It would be more suitable for donors to bolster local expertise by developing vocational schools and university-level training courses for Libyans. These steps could guarantee a long-term source of local talent development and reduce dependency on external expertise.

Though full-scale change is in the hands of the Libyan state, donors can still hope to be a positive actor in the process.

POWER PLAYS

The struggle of farmers against the desert in the sleepy town of Brak al-Shati, 400 miles south of Tripoli, rarely attracts external attention. But the town made national headlines in 2019 when armed individuals forced their way into the Great Man-Made River (GMMR) control center in the south and forced technicians to switch off the system, effectively cutting off water access for several cities in Libya including Tripoli's 1 million residents.

Muammar al-Gaddafi referred to the GMMR as "the eighth wonder of the world" when its construction began in the 1980s, and it remains the world's largest irrigation project. Libya uses the GMMR to extract and transport groundwater from southern Libya to cities around the country. But some towns, such as Brak al-Shati, do not have access to GMMR pipelines, instead depending on electricity to pump water from local aquifers.

The group was attempting to pressure the political elite to restore electricity to cities and towns in the south. This act of sabotage was intended to prove a point—while electricity cuts are common across the country, they are especially debilitating in Brak al-Shati where a loss of power means a loss of water, and without either, life comes to a halt.

Similar tactics have been used in Libya, such as when local armed groups attacked GECOL power plants to protest loadshedding schedules that impacted their neighborhoods. But these actions can sometimes backfire. Instead of improving electricity provision for their communities, interruptions to an already fragile grid can result in a total system shutdown that plunges entire cities into total darkness.

Source: Matthew Brubacher, "Moving to a sunnier future," *The World Today*, December 2019 and January 2020, https://www.chathamhouse.org/publications/the-world-today/2019-12/why-libya-should-be-soaking-sun; Michael Cousins, "Water trickles back but week-long water stoppage has effected millions," *Libya Herald*, December 4, 2017, https://www.libyaherald.com/2017/12/water-slowly-trickles-back-but-week-long-water-stoppage-has-affected-millions/; Jehad Nasir, "مؤسسة ليبية تأسف لاستمرار انقطاع مياه الشرب عن العاصمة خلال العيد" [A Libyan institution regrets the continued interruption of drinking water from the capital during Eid], Anadolu Agency, August 13, 2019, https://bit.ly/2ORrkmJ; "براك الشاطئ.. ما بين سوء الخدمات وغلاء الأسعار" [Brak Al Shati .. between poor services and high prices], 218tv, July 5, 2020, http://bit.ly/3YOFkwK; and "جنود الشركة العامة للكهرباء يتعرضون للاعتداء في المنطقة الجنوبية" [General Electricity Company employees are being attacked in the southern region], Ean Libya, June 17, 2019, http://bit.ly/3Ipvwnr.

-/AFP via Getty Images

YEMEN OPPORTUNITY AMID COLLAPSE

Iman Ghaleb Hadi al-Hamali used to go to bed at 7:00 p.m.[196] The 35-year-old woman lived 20 miles from the front lines of the conflict in rural northern Yemen and could not afford the fuel she needed to generate electricity. With no power, there was nothing to do after nightfall. Like most of her neighbors, she decided she might as well go to bed.

But now, Iman stays busy late into the evening. She leads a group of 10 women who manage a solar-powered micro-grid and sell cheaper and cleaner power to villagers. The UNDP provided seed money and trained the women to manage the micro-grid.[197]

At first, Iman's male relatives and neighbors opposed the project and mocked the women, but the benefits of reliable power are now clear to the whole community: electricity is up to 65 percent cheaper than that obtained from diesel generators, children can study after dark, entrepreneurs have invested in electric tools and set up businesses, and the experience has inspired other women to enter the workforce. Iman now plans to reinvest her profits to expand the system to other neighborhoods in her district.

Iman's story is a rare success. Yemen is experiencing a severe electricity crisis that has left millions without affordable and reliable power. The public grid collapsed in northern areas controlled by the Houthi movement and is very weak in most of the areas controlled by the Internationally Recognized Government of Yemen (IRG). In the absence of direction from the state, the sector has fragmented and exacerbated inequalities. Unlike Iman's well-maintained solar micro-grid, many Yemenis rely on generators that use dirty fuel oil or poor-quality rooftop solar panels.

Donors have provided emergency assistance to some critical infrastructure, including hospitals, water pumping stations, and schools, to mitigate the worst effects of the electricity collapse. However, the fear of ongoing instability and challenges of working with central authorities have deterred them from attempting more major development interventions in the electricity sector.

Iman's solar micro-grid suggests that there may be a window of opportunity in Yemen for donors to catalyze positive change and create wide-reaching benefits. In comparison to the other countries in this study, there is more space for donors to experiment with new systems of electricity provision because vested interests are weaker in Yemen and local politics are more conducive to change. Centralized control over the electricity sector has fragmented during the conflict, and no actor enjoys a monopoly over fuel imports or the generation, transmission, or provision of electricity in Yemen. The absence of a monopoly creates space for experimentation with alternative systems of electricity provision.

Conditions in northern Yemen are most conducive to a distributed system of renewable energy. The Houthis have never controlled major electricity infrastructure and are more open to alternative systems. They have an incentive to advance renewable energy because it facilitates economic recovery, and they can charge fees on the import of renewable technologies. Distributed systems of renewable energy also enjoy a high level of public receptiveness and are appropriate for the mountainous terrain. In areas of Houthi

"

Iman's solar micro-grid suggests that there may be a window of opportunity in Yemen for donors to catalyze positive change and create wide-reaching benefits.

Major Electricity Infrastructure and Zones of Control in Yemen

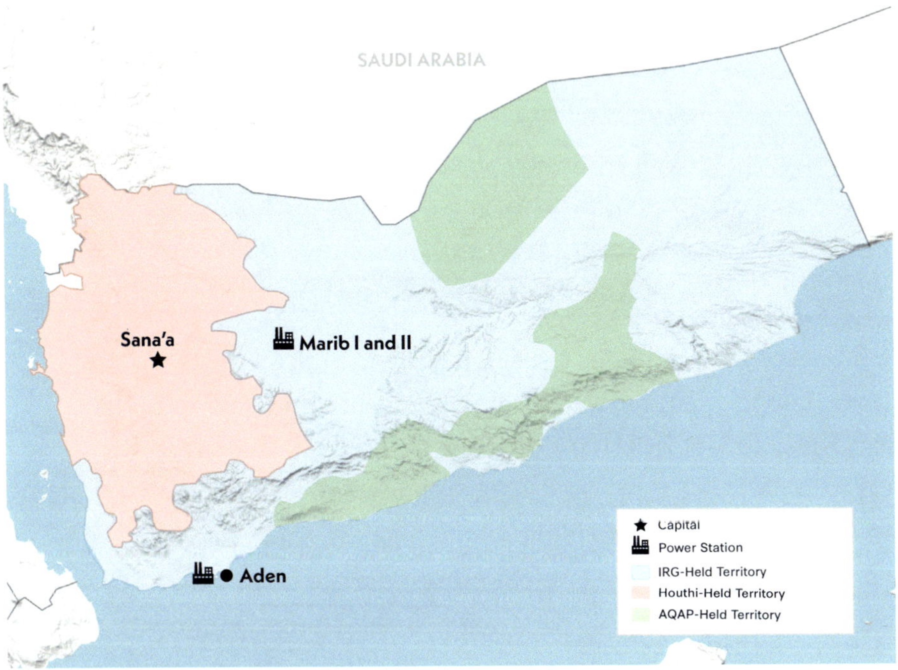

Source: Adapted from "Yemen," Live Universal Awareness Map, https://yemen.liveuamap.com/.

control, the population does not have a history of relying on central state authorities for electricity and are therefore more willing to turn to private or local solutions.

In IRG-held areas, some actors have an economic interest in the dysfunctional status quo and work to obstruct the transition to more economically and environmentally sustainable systems of electricity provision. Private generator owners have amassed influence and profit from the short-term contracts they have with the government to provide power, which the government repeatedly renews. The population in IRG-held areas also expects the government to provide cheap power for them due to the legacy of the socialist government. However, more openings for change exist in these areas than in other countries covered in this study. The government has an interest in reducing its significant losses in the electricity sector and is exploring alternative ways to provide electricity.

The openness of central authorities to local systems of electricity provision creates exciting opportunities for donors to advance a new system before networks of corruption take hold. A distributed system would reduce opportunities for corruption by reducing reliance on regular imports of fuel. Donors could help unlock climate financing to expand and scale up distributed renewable energy systems and utility-scale projects, setting Yemen on a path to greater economic and environmental sustainability while also reducing the likelihood of corrupt actors cementing their control over the electricity sector in the future.

PRIOR WEAKNESS

Prior to the current conflict, Yemen already had the weakest electricity sector in the region.[198] Just 40 percent of households were connected to the state grid, and less than 60 percent of the population had access to electricity at all, whether from the state or private off-grid systems. There was a stark divide between those living in urban and rural areas, with electricity reaching 85 percent of the urban population but just 23 percent of rural communities, which is where more than two-thirds of the population lived.[199] The situation grew progressively worse as the government's efforts to expand electricity access failed to keep up with population growth and increasing demand.

Furthermore, the electricity sector was poorly managed. The Ministry of Electricity and Energy (MoEE) was responsible for setting policy and strategic plans, while the Public Electricity Corporation (PEC) was the sole electricity supplier and the utility responsible for managing generation, transmission, distribution, and bill collection. The PEC managed outdated and inefficient power plants, and more than 40 percent of generated electricity was lost in transmission and distribution.[200] The PEC also relied on transfers from the government, as it failed to collect enough money to cover its costs. While the government made ambitious plans to integrate renewables into its energy mix in 2009, it had made little progress before the war.[201] International donors did not yet view renewables as a priority and had provided little funding for the projects. Prior to the war, Yemen had no utility-scale renewable energy projects.

The government expressed interest in reforming the sector but struggled to overcome public resistance to change. In 2009, it passed a law that set the stage for reforms in the electricity sector by unbundling the PEC, splitting it into three entities, and establishing an independent regulator. However, some of the PEC's 30,000 employees fiercely opposed the reforms and threatened to stage protests.[202] As the Arab Spring protests reached Yemen in 2011, the poor state of electricity provision became a flashpoint. The Government of National Reconciliation tried to reform the electricity sector as part of the Mutual Accountability Framework that it established with international donors, but the reforms it proposed received strong opposition. After the government cut subsidies in 2014, the Houthis staged mass sit-ins in Sana'a.

However, the PEC never had a full monopoly, and private-sector engagement in Yemen's electricity system dates back decades. During the 1970s, migrants from the Yemen Arab Republic who worked in Saudi Arabia invested in community-scale generators and sold electricity to their neighbors in northern Yemen.[203] In 2006, the government began to rely on the private sector as well. The PEC contracted with privately owned generators to cover electricity shortfalls, and the government provided the generators with subsidized fuel. This strategy helped attract private investment, but it placed considerable strain on government budgets. Contracts to the private sector were intended to be a short-term measure, but absent improvements to electricity supply, the government continued to renew them.

International actors attempted to build Yemen's central capacity for electricity generation prior to the conflict, and Arab Gulf states provided the most significant support. The Arab Fund for Economic and Social Development and the Saudi Fund for Development provided funding for Siemens and the Arabian Bemco Contracting group to construct a 342 MW power station in Marib, Yemen's first gas-fired power plant, commissioned in 2009.[204] The same two donors also funded the Marib II gas power plant, Yemen's largest, and construction began in 2014.[205] Various Gulf donors and the World Bank also pledged $144 million in funding for Yemen to build its first wind farm in Mocha in 2014.[206] Meanwhile, donors also pursued projects to expand electricity access to rural areas. A coalition of donors agreed to a $118 million electrification project in 12 rural areas across 12 governorates to support on-grid and off-grid communities.[207] However, growing instability and the outbreak of fighting forced donors to suspend all of these projects.

THE CURRENT CRISIS

The government lost control of the electricity sector when conflict broke out. The conflict halted the government's strategic initiatives, exacerbated inequalities in electricity access, and left the sector in chaos. The war damaged 55 percent of Yemen's electricity infrastructure and destroyed another 8 percent of it completely.[208] Most damage was in Houthi-controlled areas in the north, which lost access to public electricity. Electricity infrastructure in the south remained largely intact, and the IRG began to operate it again in late 2015. Today, most consumers connected to the grid in IRG-held areas still receive some state power each day, although the amount varies significantly by governorate.[209]

The conflict brought an abrupt halt to international donors' development projects. The Gulf-funded Marib I power plant, the primary source of power for Houthi-controlled areas, went offline in May 2015 after a break in the circuit between Marib and Sana'a. Work on the Marib II power plant and the Mocha wind farm project was also halted, and the World Bank abandoned its rural electrification project, having made little progress.

The infrastructure that remained intact was increasingly difficult to operate. Shortages in fossil fuels forced operators to take power stations offline, and the loss of human capital and data undermined the management of the sector. When many government agencies moved from Sana'a to Aden in 2015, they were unable to take their records with them.[210] With increasing illegal connections and challenges with bill collection, the PEC's financial struggles increased, and the government was forced to lift electricity subsidies.

Yemen's electricity crisis has had cascading humanitarian effects. The lack of reliable and affordable electricity has exacerbated crises in water access and food insecurity and further undermined the healthcare and education sectors.

The IRG is now unable to direct the electricity sector. The PEC has fragmented, and the government has halted its strategic plans and struggles to conduct even basic maintenance to the grid due to financial losses. Under pressure from public and private interests, the IRG quickly abandoned its reform agenda. It reinstated subsidies and renewed contracts with private electricity providers, which are skewed in favor of the generator owners. The government pays them according to generators' capacity rather than power produced or consumed, meaning that owners are paid in full even if the government cannot provide them with fuel. As such, they have no incentive to produce more electricity or make their fuel consumption more efficient.[211] As one Yemeni analyst noted, "Private power providers' strength is evident from the fact that the government has not been able to improve the terms of the contracts."[212]

Meanwhile, the Houthis rapidly implemented many of the reforms to the electricity sector that the government had previously resisted. Just a year after staging a sit-in to protest the Hadi government's decision to lift subsidies, the Houthis themselves eliminated fuel subsidies. Prices spiked and consumers began to pay up to 10 times more than they did before the war, but the Houthis then implemented a price cap for electricity and regulated the privatization of electricity provision.[213] The Houthis started to rent out state electricity infrastructure, such as distribution lines, to private sector actors. They also delegated the generation and distribution of electricity from remaining public stations to a company owned by a close associate. "They essentially implemented all the reforms we had been pushing for," a Yemeni development expert said, "but not in the way we imagined."[214]

Several factors have enabled the Houthis to implement reforms to the electricity sector, while the IRG has returned to its old habits. Private electricity providers have resisted IRG's attempts to reform in the south, but they lack leverage over the Houthis in the north. When the Houthis came to power, they did not have strong social or political ties with private actors in the electricity sector, allowing them to circumvent preexisting business interests. Likewise, Yemenis in the north were more accustomed to private sector activity than those in the south, which had a purely socialist system from 1967 to 1990 and which relied on government provision to a greater extent.[215] As a result, Yemenis in the north had less expectation of cheap government service and turned to their own electricity solutions more readily.

"

The lack of reliable and affordable electricity has exacerbated crises in water access and food insecurity and further undermined the healthcare and education sectors.

OPPORTUNITIES FOR RENEWABLES

Yemenis have turned to solar power as their primary adaptation measure. Solar power was already being used in some rural communities before the conflict, but the war motivated an important expansion of solar power in urban areas as well. The spread of solar energy, particularly in northern Yemen, indicates a relatively permissive political environment for innovation in the sector. In 2019, 75 percent of households with access to electricity across Yemen used solar home systems as their primary source of power.[216]

Solar technology spread in two main phases. In the first phase, individual households led the transition, as citizens who were able to afford solar technology installed it on their rooftops as a strategy of self-reliance. In the second phase, donors fueled the spread of solar for key infrastructure and institutions, such as water pumping, schools, and hospitals.

The grassroots spread of solar technology faces several key challenges. The lack of institutional capacity means that there is no regulation of the market and insufficient skilled labor to operate and maintain the technology. With no national standards, poor-quality technology has spread throughout the country. For example, some users repurpose truck batteries rather than using dedicated batteries for solar power. One NGO worker said, "Some equipment that should have lasted for 25 years has broken after just a couple of years."[217] These problems have led many Yemenis to turn to private neighborhood generators as a more reliable source of power, maintaining their solar systems as a back-up measure.[218]

Yemenis have also struggled to import solar technology through various zones of control. The Saudi-led coalition's air and sea blockade of Yemen has led to some difficulties in importing solar technology and has raised costs. One NGO worker noted that "Importers have to pay several sets of customs duties when equipment passes through different areas of control."[219] Another key obstacle to the grassroots spread of renewable technology has been the lack of financing options for consumers. Many Yemenis have very low incomes, and there are no financial mechanisms to encourage uptake of renewable technology.

Despite these challenges, economic and political incentives encourage the uptake of renewable energy. Yemen's reliance on expensive fuel imports and its inability to use its own hydrocarbon reserves for electricity generation mean that many political groups have an interest in adopting less fuel-intensive systems of electricity generation. While fuel imports have historically been subject to profiteering in Yemen, the government's monopoly over fuel imports collapsed during the conflict, and private actors are now able to import fuel.[220] Although many of these private importers have links to political elites across different zones of control and continue to profit from commissions on imports, increased competition over fuel imports has fractured their ability to control the market.

Central authorities have no interest in stopping the spread of renewable technologies. For the IRG, reducing the number of people who rely on the public grid is a way to reduce their financial losses in the sector. PEC officials in various parts of Yemen expressed interest in exploring renewable energy in interviews, calling for feasibility studies and small-scale pilot projects, such as mini-grids.[221] Similarly, the Houthis have no incentive to block the spread of renewable energy, as their ability to profit from the provision of electricity is more limited given the destruction of state infrastructure. They benefit to a limited extent from solar technology because they can charge traders fees to import solar equipment.[222]

Although private generator owners seek to maintain their profits and have reportedly been behind some attacks on the public grid, there is significant competition between

> "Central authorities have no interest in **stopping the spread of renewable technologies.**

them. In Sana'a alone, there are more than 260 commercial diesel generator companies.[223] The Houthis' price cap on the amount private providers can charge for electricity has also limited opportunities to exploit customers in the sector.[224] And the lifting of fuel subsidies means that these generator owners have an incentive to reduce their reliance on fuel, creating an opening to encourage them to integrate solar panels into their systems.[225]

DONOR STRATEGIES

Because of the permissive political environment and Yemenis' acute need for energy, there are few restrictions on the type of projects donors can implement in the electricity sector in Yemen. However, their interventions have been limited to date. Donors are funding targeted humanitarian interventions to support critical infrastructure with renewable energy but have not articulated a concerted strategy to develop the sector.

Donors can shape local projects with relative freedom, coordinating with local authorities rather than with IRG officials.[226] Local leaders, such as branches of water and health authorities, local councils, and tribal heads, have a strong incentive to encourage development projects in their regions. Whereas donors delivered some funds through the Ministry of Finance and other government bodies before the war, now donors mainly funnel funds through international organizations and have limited interactions with ministries.[227] However, their freedom of project selection is not evenly distributed across Yemen. International actors tend to focus on rural areas because authorities in urban areas have more influence, attempt to shape project design, and try to determine beneficiaries.[228] In northern Yemen, the Houthis established the Supreme Council for the Management and Coordination of Humanitarian Affairs and International Cooperation, which approves organizations' interventions and supervises their work.

Despite the challenging security and political environment in Yemen, UN agencies have managed to implement electricity projects across 20 of Yemen's 21 governorates, spanning different areas of control.[229] These interventions demonstrate donors' ability to intervene across the country and help counter accusations of political bias.

The most successful renewable energy interventions have been replacing diesel water pumps for households, facilities, and

"

UN agencies have managed to implement electricity projects across 20 of Yemen's 21 governorates, spanning different areas of control.

farms with solar-powered pumps.[230] These interventions have been critical for supplying drinking water and should be encouraged for domestic use. However, in some cases, solar-powered irrigation systems have allowed farmers to overexploit water resources.[231]

Other internationally funded renewable projects have supported medical facilities and schools. Solar systems have helped hospitals and clinics reduce their reliance on diesel. However, these systems must be based on a hybrid power supply because some medical equipment, such as that used in surgery departments, requires constant, high levels of energy. The World Bank has also collaborated with microfinance institutions to distribute subsidized pico-solar systems through a UN Office for Project Services project. Pico solar-electric systems are very small, mobile systems of electricity generation, which allow Yemenis to charge phones and operate some small tools.

Yemeni interviewees criticized the unsustainability of some of these projects. Donors often invest in infrastructure and hope that local institutions or communities will take responsibility for operations and maintenance. However, when they fail to do so and when donors refuse to provide additional support, these projects can fail and turn local communities against renewable energy. These are also piecemeal measures that do not represent a comprehensive solution to electricity problems.

The most impactful donor intervention in the electricity sector has provided a short-term boost but is not sustainable.[232] In 2021, the Saudi Development and Reconstruction Program granted the IRG $422 million in petroleum products to operate 80 power stations across Yemen.[233] Saudi Arabia has since provided a second grant, and discussions are ongoing about the possibility of a third. However, this support is only provided to areas controlled by the IRG, which exacerbates inequalities and the politicization of the electricity sector.[234] It is also a short-term and unsustainable solution that fails to build long-term resilience in the electricity sector.

CONCLUSION: VARYING CENTRAL CAPACITY AND LIMITED INTERESTS IN THE STATUS QUO

Conditions are right to explore more widespread deployment of renewable energy technologies in Yemen. Donors are right to continue to support critical humanitarian infrastructure, but they should now expand the volume and scope of community-scale projects and some larger-scale projects to build the resilience of Yemen's electricity sector. A window of opportunity exists to accelerate Yemen's transition to sustainability and expand its resilience.

Renewable energy has become the most affordable source of electricity in Yemen. Imported diesel and heavy fuel oil is expensive, and although Yemen has gas reserves and its largest power plant is gas-fired, it is not currently a viable option for electricity generation because the plant is located close to the front lines and gas infrastructure has been destroyed. Yemen's geography and large rural population mean a centralized grid is not the most efficient way to serve its energy needs. Additionally, Yemen has one of the world's highest solar yields and also has significant potential for wind energy. There are also few spoilers in Yemen who would be able to block the expansion of renewable energy, as no actor has a monopoly over the electricity sector and the sector is comparatively free of corruption.[235]

Donors should pursue different types of projects in different parts of Yemen and avoid generalizations about the difficulty of working in Yemen. As one Yemeni development expert noted, "donors write all of Yemen off as being too unstable for development interventions," adding that donors' lack of appetite for risk constrains their willingness to pursue more creative interventions.[236] Although some areas remain unstable and major work on infrastructure rehabilitation would be unwise, other parts of Yemen have not seen major violence and are much safer. In these more stable areas, donors should support feasibility studies for utility-scale wind and solar installations and help attract private investment. Renewable energy technology could also be explored for smaller-scale desalination and wastewater treatment units.

Donors can also build on the success of Iman al-Hamali's micro-grid by supporting larger community-scale renewable and hybrid projects for off-grid populations, particularly in rural areas, and allowing other communities to replicate the model. For example, donors should conduct a feasibility study into a mini-grid of 1 MW or more, which could prove more financially viable due to economies of scale. Donors should encourage the UNDP to release the feasibility studies for its micro-grid projects and details about the business model so that other communities can attract investment to replicate the success. The UNDP has not yet released these details

"

There are also few spoilers in Yemen who would be able to block the expansion of renewable energy.

while the project is ongoing and before it has completed a full evaluation.[237] Donors should also explore ways to incentivize the owners of private mini-grids to hybridize their systems by integrating solar panels.

To pursue these goals, donors will need to find ways to boost private sector investment in the sector. Donors should identify capital subsidies and engage with green funds to encourage them to end their hesitation to provide support to Yemen. Donors should also explore the feasibility of providing guarantees to private investors since the Yemeni government is unable to do so.

The benefits of advancing the share of renewable electricity in the energy mix would be wide-reaching. First, it would enhance energy security while supporting the resilience of energy infrastructure and reducing reliance on expensive and dirty imported fuel. Second, it would provide communities with cascading benefits by bolstering local economic development. Third, it would capitalize on the window of opportunity to fast-track progress toward Yemen's climate goals. And perhaps most significantly for the purposes of this study, it would help avoid the entrenchment of graft in the electricity sector, as has happened in other conflict-affected states in the region.

LUDOVIC MARIN/AFP via Getty Images

BUILDING BACK BETTER

POWER AND REFORM

International donors have pursued a failing approach to rebuilding electricity sectors in conflict-affected states in the Middle East. From Iraq, to Lebanon, to Yemen, they pushed for reforms and made huge investments in major power stations that were intended to serve millions of people in need.

However, time and time again, these investments have failed to fix the problems that they sought to address, and reforms often failed to materialize. For example, in Iraq, donors helped Siemens win a contract to provide a gas turbine for a large power plant at Baiji. In 2014, the plant had just been completed when the ISG destroyed it. Nearly a decade later, it remains offline.

In Lebanon, donors provided over $100 million toward the construction of the Zahrani power station. In 2022, Lebanon's lack of fuel forced it offline.[238] In Yemen, the donor-funded Marib power plant has been offline since 2015, yet the instinct of donors has once again been to fund new thermal power stations.[239] Though these multimillion-dollar investments are risky and have not fixed electricity problems in other conflict-affected environments in the region, donors continue down the same path.

Donors prefer this approach for several reasons. Rehabilitating existing infrastructure is cost-effective, relatively quick, and facilitates the entry of international energy companies, with which some donor governments enjoy close ties. It is easier for donors to vet and administer a few major contracts than hundreds of small ones, and they likewise believe such arrangements make it easier to monitor how money is spent. However, this strategy often has the effect of entrenching local elites who control the infrastructure and who have an interest in ongoing dysfunction. The alternative, a concerted effort to condition aid on deep reforms, runs head-on into ruling elites' interests. They have a wide range of political tools, ranging from legislative obstruction to public protest to violence, that they can, and often do, use to block reform. In Iraq, Lebanon, Libya, and Yemen, political elites have resisted external efforts to establish independent regulators for the electricity sector, have maintained electricity subsidies for as long as they can, and have failed to improve tariff collection measures. This resistance to reform undermines donors' efforts to promote stability and exit from the reconstruction process. The cost of inaction while donors wait for reforms is also high, as poor electricity provision increases the costs of interventions in other sectors, including water provision, healthcare, and education.

To improve electricity provision in conflict-affected environments, donors need to draw inspiration from local adaptations, act more quickly, and think more politically. To address humanitarian and governance issues concurrently, donors must seize on the window of opportunity before political and economic actors develop an interest in a dysfunctional electricity sector. Local initiatives that provide electricity at the community level demonstrate the opportunity to do things differently. Donors should identify success stories, assess how they navigated the conflict-affected contexts, and explore the feasibility of scaling up such innovative solutions. Donors can then nurture these initiatives and grow them into something bigger by helping to replicate them, sharing best practices, and enabling change on a larger scale. Doing so requires an exploration of ways to co-opt, circumvent, and coerce potential spoilers. This strategy would facilitate the provision of more reliable, cheaper, and cleaner electricity, which will bring economic, security, political, and environmental benefits and make savings for donors in many other sectors.

To address humanitarian and governance issues concurrently, donors must seize on the window of opportunity before political and economic actors develop an interest in a dysfunctional electricity sector.

To predict the viability of interventions that advance renewable energy in conflict-affected environments, donors must assess the contours of the political economy and the elasticity of the political environment in the early recovery period.

Several aspects of a political economy work against the expansion of alternative systems of electricity provision. Subsidies are a key obstacle, especially in the MENA region. States such as Iraq and Libya that provide generous subsidies for electricity provision not only deter investment in alternatives but also discourage consumers from rationalizing their energy consumption. A common assumption is that popular opposition and the risk of protest prevents governments from raising electricity tariffs, but some elites do not want subsidies dismantled because it would allow for the entry of other actors into the electricity sectors that would challenge elite monopolies and limit their ability to profit.

> **To address humanitarian and governance issues concurrently, donors must seize on the window of opportunity before political and economic actors develop an interest in a dysfunctional electricity sector.**

ASSESSING RIPENESS FOR REFORM

However, economic crises force governments in many conflict-affected states to raise electricity tariffs. Authorities in both Lebanon and Yemen lifted electricity subsidies as a result of their current crises. Although the results are devastating for consumers, these crises create conditions that are more conducive to diversifying the electricity sector and advancing renewables.

Hydrocarbon resources also deter reform. Oil and gas revenues in Iraq and Libya have cushioned the governments from economic crises, allowed them to continue to subsidize failing electricity sectors, and contributed to citizens' unwillingness to pursue renewable technology. In Baghdad, the owner of a small solar energy company said, "Lots of potential customers tell me that Iraq has the fifth-largest proven hydrocarbon reserves in the world and think it is the government's duty to provide them with affordable electricity."[240] The irony, as he noted, is that many Iraqis pay hundreds of dollars to private generator owners each month because the government is unable to provide the service they expect.

The presence of local adaptations that provide alternative supplies of electricity using renewables demonstrates the possibility to do things differently. Even without large levels of foreign support, these initiatives have spread throughout Lebanon and Yemen; at the same time, they remain rare in Iraq and Libya, where high energy subsidies and hydrocarbon wealth limit the space for experimentation and communities' receptivity to alternative systems. Donor interventions are therefore more likely to be effective in conflict-affected environments where there are not high energy subsidies and where governments do not enjoy hydrocarbon wealth.

Next, donors should determine when to intervene. When conflicts uproot the political order, they create new windows of opportunity for change. In Yemen, the Houthis implemented many of the reforms that international donors called for in the electricity sector, in part because they were new to power and were not constrained by preexisting networks of patronage that could have limited their freedom of action. They have a political interest in increasing electricity access to boost their legitimacy and have not yet developed strong connections with private generator owners from which they can profit.

Iraq and Lebanon highlight the danger of waiting too long. Elites have worked together to obstruct reforms that would expand renewable technologies and limit their profits. Over recent decades, Iraqi and Lebanese political elites have spent billions of dollars in the electricity sector to prevent the entry of competitors.

These experiences suggest that donor interventions are more likely to catalyze change if they act in the early recovery phase rather than waiting for the crystallization of a new political settlement and the entrenchment of political and business interests that favor dysfunction.

WIELDING LEVERAGE

Having ascertained that there is an openness to reform, donors must seek ways to maximize the impact of their interventions in the electricity sector. On the central level, donors can condition reconstruction assistance on reforms that will enable more sustainable electricity provision and limit the entrenchment of interests that favor dysfunction. Such reforms include drafting legal frameworks to enable the expansion of renewable energy, establishing independent regulatory authorities to enforce standards, and implementing energy tariff reforms to encourage investment in renewables. Donor governments and international financial institutions must make any large-scale assistance contingent on these reforms. For example, the IMF should mainstream these reforms in the conditionality of its loan package for Lebanon.

However, aid conditionality alone will not achieve these reforms. The Lebanese political elite's resistance to reforms in the electricity sector for more than 20 years demonstrates the limits of aid leverage. Donors must therefore work to understand the winners and losers of proposed reforms, align incentives, and build coalitions that have an interest in seeing the desired changes.[241] Local analysts are often best placed to understand the costs and benefits of reforms on different political actors. Donors should support them to produce independent analyses that can inform their strategies.

It is also critical to engage citizens in the reform process. Coalition building requires clear evidence of the costs of the status quo and the benefits of adopting a new system of electricity provision, including credible pricing forecasts.[242] Donors should sequence reforms in a way that minimizes the pain to consumers, focuses on demand-side reforms that benefit consumers, and builds citizens' belief that they will benefit from reforms.[243] For example, they should focus on mitigating technical and nontechnical losses in the electricity sector to boost provision before hiking energy tariffs.

Donors should assess when obstacles to reform are political or bureaucratic. In many conflict-affected environments, public sectors are debilitated by a loss of human capital through brain drain and limited resources. A Lebanese state utility official warned that the country is operating in dire conditions with a fraction of its workforce, asking "Even if leadership agreed to reforms, who would implement them?"[244] Donors should provide technical and legal assistance to governments to implement reforms when necessary. Providing this support removes actors' ability to claim that they have insufficient capacity to enact reforms and makes clear when political or business interests are the true cause of inaction. The Lebanon Reform, Recovery and Reconstruction Framework (3RF), established by the European Union, the United Nations, and the World Bank in response to the 2020 Beirut port explosion, provides a model for this strategy. 3RF incorporates and institutionalizes civil society actors in high-level policy discussions between international donors and the Lebanese government through their membership of consultative groups.[245] They can provide technical insights to ensure that reform discussions are grounded in reality.

Donors must limit the possibility of their reconstruction activities creating new opportunities for corruption. In recent years, whistleblowers have raised alarm about corruption in energy and environmental projects implemented by UN agencies. For example, one whistleblower, John O'Brien, raised concerns that a UNDP energy efficiency program in Russia was an avenue for money laundering, and another, James Wasserstrom, found evidence that UN officials in Kosovo might have received bribes for awarding a power station contract.[246] Donors should collaborate through multilateral working groups to establish common anticorruption standards in any infrastructure projects they fund. Rather than creating independent anti-corruption agencies, which elite networks can coopt, donors should focus on supporting citizen-based monitoring and work with civil society.[247] However, this work is often dangerous for local actors, and donors should only engage civil society if they can protect local actors from retaliation.

Bidding for infrastructure projects must be competitive, and donors should award contracts on the basis of merit. Understanding the complex web of ties between political figures, their business networks, and other affiliated entities requires deep local knowledge.[248] Again, donors must provide sufficient support (and protection) to civil society actors to probe these relationships.

The pace of the distribution of international aid in the electricity sector is also significant. Corruption is often worst when donors inject large amounts of aid over a short period and then rapidly pull back. These conditions motivate corrupt actors to compete over dwindling resources, which can prompt the return of conflict.[249] This reality provides an added incentive for donors to support decentralized infrastructure.

GOING LOCAL: ISLANDS OF RESILIENCE AND A QUIET REVOLUTION

The chaos of conflict and stubbornness of central elites means that conditions are not always ripe for top-down reforms. Donors should also explore opportunities at the local level. Two of the winners of the 2019 Nobel Prize for Economics, Abhijit Banerjee and Esther Duflo, argue that marginal reforms hold more promise of development success than large plans. They conclude that "A careful understanding of the motivations and constraints of everyone . . . can lead to policies and institutions that are better designed and less likely to be perverted by corruption or dereliction of duty. These changes will be incremental, but they will sustain and build on themselves. They can be the start of a quiet revolution."[250]

Donors can push a quiet revolution by building on local adaptations, tapping into unexploited reservoirs of social capital, and exploiting the potential of off-grid renewable systems such as mini-grids. These solutions are often second-best because they are smaller scale and still require careful planning.[251] Donors have a strong preference to provide a small number of large value grants, which limits the number of actors with which they must coordinate. However, successful local projects can represent "islands of resilience" and can prepare constituencies for change by demonstrating the potential of alternative systems.

Islands of resilience are institutions that perform despite being in an environment of dysfunction or endemic corruption. They are usually self-contained institutions with a specific mandate, which they fulfil with considerably lower levels of corruption and dysfunction in comparison to other institutions in the same context.[252] The potential of these positive cases to catalyze broader change lies in their ability to inspire others.[253] They provide opportunities to transfer knowledge about success against the odds to others in the wider community. This information transfer can then motivate members of the wider community to reevaluate their current situation. Realizing they have access to the same resources as their more successful peers, they then seek to replicate the best practices.[254] This phenomenon played out in the Arab Spring, as activists emulated the strategies and tactics of first movers in other countries who faced similar constraints.[255] And the benefit of a positive example may go beyond replication to even drive experimentation. Studies on "positive deviant cases" in development show that knowledge of one innovation in a challenging context can motivate other innovations.[256]

Amplifying local islands of resilience in the electricity sector would require some shifts in donor behavior. Donors would likely need to circumvent central authorities to implement these local projects, instead working with representatives of local governments,

> **"Donors can push a quiet revolution by building on local adaptations, tapping into unexploited reservoirs of social capital, and exploiting the potential of off-grid renewable systems such as mini-grids.**

institutions, and businesses. This approach would not be entirely new. In Iraq, Lebanon, Libya, and Yemen, some donors have funded distributed systems of renewable electricity generation for key institutions and certain communities. However, an approach entirely driven by local efforts would represent a major shift for other donors, including the World Bank, which are either mandated to deal with central governments or which value the relative efficiency of addressing national needs in a single negotiation. However, departing from this practice would demonstrate the potential of a system of electricity provision that could inspire others.

A successful local model of electricity provision that integrates renewable energy, such as the women-led solar micro-grid in rural northern Yemen, serves several purposes. It is cleaner, often more affordable, and more reliable than common conflict adaptations, such as subscriptions to neighborhood diesel generators. Local projects are also more likely to build trust with local authorities and achieve community buy-in, decreasing the risk of theft or sabotage. They demonstrate that electricity problems are man-made and changeable. Even if a local solution is idiosyncratic, it illustrates the possibility of an alternative system.

Local examples can boost awareness about the potential of renewable energy in environments where it has little uptake, such as Iraq or Libya. In Lebanon, some community-based hybrid grids have prompted other communities to seek to replicate their success and build on it. The mayor of al-Ain in the Bekaa Valley has attempted to engage with international donors to gain support for a larger solar energy park after seeing the success of a solar-powered mini-grid in neighboring Jabbouleh.[257]

GOING GREEN WITH ENVY

Private investors looking to advance renewable energy in Lebanon found a willing partner in a group of nuns in the Bekaa Valley. The convent in Jabbouleh leased some of its land as part of a $1.8 million contract to establish a hybrid mini-grid managed by a private company. Thanks to the project, 340 households in Jabbouleh subscribed and now receive more reliable energy.

When residents of al-Ain municipality heard that their neighbors in Jabbouleh had continuous electricity, they tasked their mayor with replicating its success. He found a partner in the Lebanese Foundation for Renewable Energy (LFRE), a local NGO. LFRE studied the viability of the land for a solar park and found large areas of unused land that are close to national transmission lines. They then hosted a town hall with 25 local municipalities from across Lebanon's political spectrum to gauge interest in a much larger project. The new alliance of municipalities voted to proceed with the project and elected the mayor of al-Ain to serve as their representative in discussions with international officials.

The mayor is convinced he can overcome any vested interests: "No politician and no generator owner could block this project. I will make them visit, see the scale of suffering, and witness the people's yearning for a green solution. I dare them to block it." Although the mayors of the 25 municipalities are lobbying their members of parliament and the minister of energy, they have not yet gained the government's approval.

The mayor approached the World Bank for funding and described plans for a hybrid solar park that could serve the needs of the 220,000 inhabitants, including 30,000 Syrian refugees. They showed title deeds to prove that the land was public and discussed how the project could proceed in phases and integrate with the national grid to serve all Lebanese. However, the World Bank has no mechanism to finance municipalities and is exploring new ways to finance local and regional projects.

Unless international donors change their approach in dysfunctional environments, they will squander opportunities to advance renewable energy by capitalizing on new forms of political association that coalesce through the desire to replicate their neighbors' success.

Source: Alix Chaplain, "Strategies of Power and the Emergence of Hybrid Mini-Grids in Lebanon," Jadaliyya, March 8, 2022, https://www.jadaliyya.com/Details/43932; author's interview with Zaccariah Nasreddin, mayor of al-Ain, Lebanon, May 23, 2022; and author's remote interview with Rony Karam, president of LFRE, February 2, 2023.

Donors' implementing partners must undertake several steps to bring about change at the local level. To begin with, they must identify veto-holders who could block a transition to a new system and that have a vested political or business interest in the status quo. Directly engaging with these actors and explaining the aims of the project may stop them from sabotaging the projects. In northern Yemen, UNDP engaged local generator owners in the first stages of their micro-grid project to explain that they were not planning to challenge their business and were implementing a smaller project.[258] Donors' implementing partners could also think about ways to make it personally advantageous for these actors to support the new system, including involving them in the new system. For example, donors could provide incentives to neighborhood generator owners in Yemen to hybridize their neighborhood grids by integrating solar panels into their grids. Although the idea of embedding grifters into the system may seem suboptimal, it would bring many advantages. It could be the cheapest option, as working with preexisting neighborhood grids would remove the need to finance an expensive new network. Including these actors would also reduce a potential source of opposition to the new system and has proven successful in parts of Lebanon.

If direct outreach to these veto-holders fails, donors should identify individuals that exert pressure over them and help build a coalition for change. These could be members of their families, communities, or tribes who have an interest in better electricity provision. In Lebanon, the management of Electricité de Zahle (EDZ) worked with businesspeople, religious groups, media personnel, and NGOs to build support for its unique concession, which allowed it to provide a higher quality of electricity service. EDZ's coalition-building strategies included offering rewards to constituents for support, but the company also worked to build local pride in the idea of Zahle having continuous power access while the rest of the country lay in darkness.[259]

The Zahle experience demonstrates the importance of tapping into underexploited sources of social capital. The shared experiences of conflict bind communities in new ways, such as collaborating on a local adaptation or taking shelter together.[260] New forms of political and social organization also emerge in the chaos of war, creating new potential partners to engage. Donors should pay particular attention to women's changing roles during times of conflict. Iman al-Hamali's solar micro-grid in Yemen shows that women can play an instrumental role

"[Donors] must identify veto-holders who could block a transition to a new system and that have a vested political or business interest in the status quo.

in managing a new system of electricity provision even in conservative societies.

Donors should experiment by supporting a range of alternative models for different communities and institutions. A solution for a densely populated neighborhood of Baghdad, which is likely to require a hybrid system, will look very different to a solution for rural Anbar province in Iraq, which could rely more heavily on solar-powered water pumps. Like in angel investing, not all investments will pay off, but there is great value in identifying context-specific solutions which can demonstrate a proof of concept. To facilitate the replication of these successful models, donors should release feasibility studies and details of the business models used so that other local investors may mimic them.

These local projects are not without risks. Smaller, more decentralized projects may avoid the risk of large-scale kickbacks, but they are still prone to rent-seeking exploitation and political influence at the local level. Decisionmaking at the municipality level may be vested in the central government or national political parties. And even if central elites are weakened and see small-scale models as a limited threat, they may still have tools to sabotage them. In Lebanon, the national utility is suing the private company that operates the Jabbouleh mini-grid in the Bekaa Valley, alleging that the system relies on the illegal use of state infrastructure.[261]

Decentralized projects also run the risk of exacerbating inequalities between communities. Rural areas are more likely to have the land required for solar parks than urban areas and so these projects will be harder to implement in cities. However, rural communities are often disadvantaged with poorer electricity access and so projects in rural areas may partially remedy preexisting inequalities. In Yemen, for example, the spread of solar systems in rural areas has helped address urban-rural inequality in electricity access.

Highlighting success stories in electricity generation in the wrong way could also lead donors to inadvertently exacerbate tensions between communities. Just as information about success stories could inspire others to replicate their experience, they could also build resentment among those who operate systems that do not receive such praise or those whose management style is tacitly criticized.[262] Including these constituencies in the identification of effective strategies and including them as partners in efforts to scale solutions up may make dissemination more likely.[263]

Another concern is the difficulty of establishing partnerships between donors and local communities. It is harder for donors to manage several small projects with local communities than a smaller number of large projects with central state authorities. An official from an international finance institution working in Yemen said that he could not launch a new project for less than $30 million.[264] Donors may also struggle to identify suitable talent among local communities to coordinate with and implement the projects.

On the other side of the equation, local communities in conflict-affected areas do not have equal opportunities to access international funding. Representatives of local communities that have ties to international donors and experience working with international bureaucracies are more likely to benefit from these opportunities. Interviewees in Lebanon suggested that the sectarian and regional backgrounds of local staff working for some donor governments and UN agencies have led to the prioritization of funding for electricity projects in certain communities over others. In Iraq, the owner of a solar company that has operated for 19 years and has 25 employees said he has given up trying to secure international funding after a few failed attempts, as he does not have the experience to fill out the applications.[265] Donors must therefore strive to implement projects across a range of geographical, sectarian, political, and economic contexts, publish transparent metrics for project selection, and seek to collaborate with new local partners whenever possible.

However, the potential benefits of local projects outweigh these risks. Once donors have identified successful models of electricity provision, they should facilitate efforts to scale them up.

BUILDING ON ISLANDS OF RESILIENCE

Islands of resilience must be publicized widely to accelerate the demand for change. Donors should support awareness campaigns that include engagement with local media, television segments, and targeted outreach to other communities. A bank manager in Iraq said, "We are sick of sad stories on the television. A story about the success of a local renewable project, with clear examples of how it benefited its community, would be the most effective way to support Iraq's electricity sector."[266] Donors can also offer prizes to innovative projects by putting out calls for local solutions.

Donors will not be able to fund many examples of these projects. They must collaborate with the private sector to unlock financing that allows for the deployment of these systems at scale in conflict-affected areas.

Climate finance is chronically underutilized in conflict-affected environments. A recent study by the International Crisis Group found that among states affected by climate change, conflict-affected countries receive a third as much climate financing per capita as those not affected by conflict.[267] The deficit of climate financing in the MENA region is especially stark, given its acute vulnerability to the effects of climate change.

A donor-led blended financing facility would be an effective way of raising sufficient funds to support large numbers of decentralized initiatives. The facility could combine donor support with private funds, including climate financing and financing from members of the diaspora. It would then provide grants, investments, seed capital, de-risking, and investment guarantees to private sector and local government actors to implement collaborative community projects. If international donors have seats on the facility's board, they could also be heavily involved in reform efforts.

These local initiatives will reduce the pressure on the central grid, help mobilize a coalition for change in the electricity sector, and help avert the entrenchment of vested interests that can block future change. By

"

Climate finance is chronically underutilized in conflict-affected environments.

seizing the window of opportunity to act on the local level, donors would have laid the groundwork for a more secure, reliable, and environmentally friendly system of electricity provision.

Support for decentralized initiatives is not a comprehensive solution for electricity provision in conflict-affected states but would be a beneficial transitional phenomenon for conflict-affected states when no alternatives exist. At some stage, central power will be reconstituted and will likely be a more effective vehicle of improving the electricity sector. But decentralized initiatives can help build linkages toward the center that facilitate that transition. Local communities must buy renewable technologies from companies that have links to businesses with central influence. These linkages can then form the sinews that hold systems together and help secure elite buy-in, as they too can gain. Over time, market forces are also likely to reward economies of scale, making multi-community and then regional-scale infrastructure more attractive. As the situation stabilizes and central authorities repair the central grid, they should provide incentives to those who manage local grids to reconnect to the main grid, including through smart-metering systems.[268]

CONCLUSION

WHAT CAN DONORS DO?

Donors' efforts to tackle electricity crises in conflict-affected states have failed. Donors are attracted to interventions that are relatively easy to administer and show clear signs of effort, but the infrastructure they traditionally build fuels corruption, creates acute vulnerabilities, and frustrates climate goals.

Multimillion-dollar thermal power stations have created major and ongoing opportunities for graft, produced dangerous single points of electricity sector failure, and tied societies to hydrocarbons, undermining the energy transition. Meanwhile, local political elites have resisted donors' reform demands, frustrating the other pillar of donors' electricity sector strategies.

The failure of these interventions has wide-reaching implications. The lack of adequate electricity stymies economic recovery from conflict, undermines the provision of essential services, and drives communal tensions. Moreover, electricity shortages exacerbate and prolong conflicts.

Innovative local adaptations demonstrate the unprecedented opportunities that new technologies are creating for providing electricity in challenging contexts. Distributed systems of electricity provision reduce opportunities for graft, build the resilience of power grids, and advance climate goals. By building on local adaptations and advancing renewable energy, international donors can achieve relatively low-cost development wins in environments that often produce high-cost losses.

Importantly, these technologies create opportunities for donors to intervene earlier in conflict-affected environments. Earlier interventions can yield much better longer-term outcomes. Donors can seize advantage of a window of opportunity to strengthen the electricity sector, power recovery, and set countries on a pathway to greater economic resilience, more effective governance, and environmental sustainability.

> **Distributed systems of electricity provision reduce opportunities for graft, build the resilience of power grids, and advance climate goals.**

PRIORITIZATION AND ACTION

Donors must have clear processes to prioritize the energy projects they support in conflict-affected environments. The priority should be to provide more reliable electricity to critical infrastructure that enables the delivery of essential services, including hospitals, water supply, wastewater collection and treatment, and schools. Another priority should be to support electricity projects that bolster food security, including by strengthening the cold chain for the safe storage and transportation of food. These interventions should limit single points of failure by building in redundancies to increase the resilience of infrastructure to withstand future shocks.

Once basic needs are met, donors should assess the feasibility of interventions in the electricity sector that foster recovery and broader economic development. Conflict conditions remain at this stage, but a short-lived window of opportunity may exist to effect change. Donors should identify local adaptations that provide electricity and learn from their success. Many local communities have found innovative ways to circumvent the challenges of the political economy and conflict conditions to provide more reliable and often cheaper electricity. Donors can serve as a force multiplier by working to strengthen these adaptations and experimenting with additional alternative systems of electricity provision. These interventions could include establishing micro-grids for rural communities, hybridizing preexisting neighborhood grids with solar panels, or even exploring the feasibility of a utility-scale solar or wind project in a more stable area.

The presence of a window of opportunity for donors to effect change at the central and local level depends on the capacity of local authorities and the intensity of vested interests in the status quo.

States with strong central governments provide a better environment for donors to pursue more major infrastructure interventions and scale up local initiatives. If central authorities maintain some ability to direct the sector and have expressed an openness to reform, it will be easier for donors to advance the integration of renewable energy into the mix. In these circumstances, donors can more easily support utility-scale renewable projects and attract interest from community groups and private sector investors to replicate successful models of distributed electricity provision. If the central government is weak, donors can still intervene at the local level but will face more challenges in replicating successful models due to the risk of investment in the unstable environment.

Donor efforts to advance renewable energy will be most successful when powerful actors do not have an interest in the status quo in the electricity sector. Various political and economic actors may have an incentive to obstruct alternative systems of electricity provision because they would lose power, influence, or profit. Hydrocarbon wealth often entrenches opportunities for graft and allows governments to fund heavy losses in the electricity sector. Similarly, powerful actors may have an interest in maintaining profit streams in the electricity sector by continuing to fund heavy energy subsidies, which reduce the viability of alternative systems of electricity provision. Donor support for renewable energy is therefore most successful in contexts where the conflict has weakened networks of cronyism and opportunities for graft in the electricity sector.

ASSESSING THE ENVIRONMENT

The following rubric provides a tool for donors to assess the presence of a window of opportunity to transform the electricity sector in a conflict-affected environment. It directs donors to assess the viability of reforms at the central level and to identify actors who are likely to obstruct the deployment of distributed renewable energy infrastructure at the local level by considering several questions. The answers can help assess government capacity and the strength of vested interests that benefit from the status quo. Once it is possible to identify which of four common environments exist in a given context, different policy recommendations follow.

First, donors should assess the capacity of central authorities as well as prospects for reform at the central level by answering several questions:

- How much electricity does the central grid provide?
- To what extent are central authorities able to manage and direct the electricity sector?
- Can authorities continue to fund energy subsidies (through hydrocarbon rents or otherwise)?
- Has any progress been made toward diversifying the energy mix?
- Does a legal framework exist for renewable energy?

Next, donors should ascertain which political actors benefit from the status quo in the electricity sector by answering another set of questions:

- To what extent are the business interests of the political elite involved in the electricity sector?
- Who controls deliveries of fuel for electricity generation (whether from domestic hydrocarbon reserves or international imports) and who profits from them?
- Do any external states have an interest in ensuring continued reliance on fuel imports?
- In what ways does state electricity rationing serve the interests of the political elite? Does the political elite provide preferential access to electricity to certain communities or industries?
- Have local communities produced their own adaptations to provide electricity?

- What are the linkages between those who benefit from informal adaptations, such as neighborhood generators, and political groups?
- Have local communities established more economically and environmentally sustainable systems of electricity provision?

The answers to these questions indicate what kind of electricity sector exists in a conflict-affected state. The emerging typology permits the identification of four types of energy sectors (see below).

Electricity Sector Categories for Donor Interventions

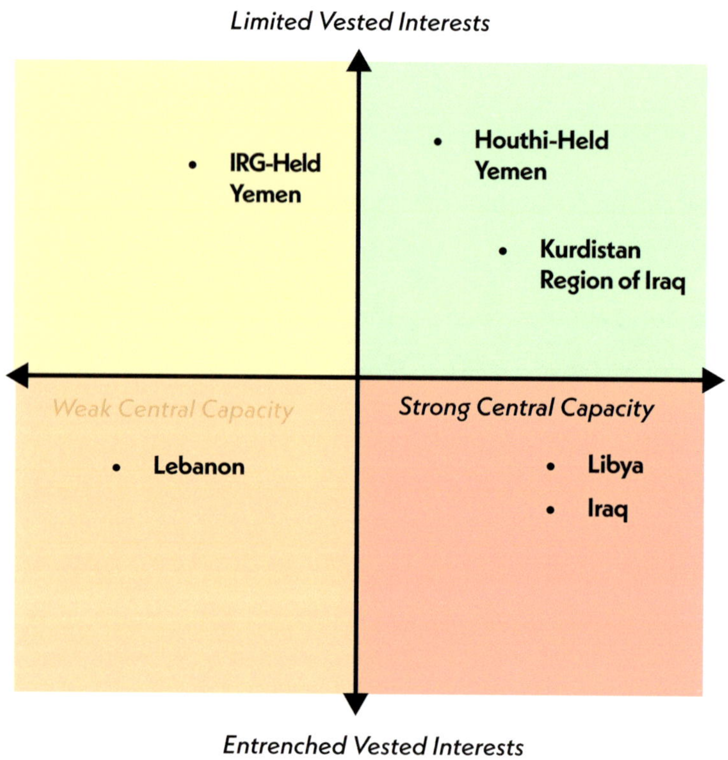

Source: Author's own creation.

STRONGER CENTRAL CAPACITY AND LIMITED VESTED INTERESTS

If the political elite does not benefit from the status quo, maintains some authority over the sector, and expresses an openness to external development assistance in the electricity sector, then donors should seize the opportunity to collaborate with the government at both the central and local levels. Donors should:

- condition support for central electricity infrastructure on reforms, such as establishing a legal framework for utility-scale and distributed renewable energy, standing up an independent electricity regulator, and implementing a tariff reform plan.
- strengthen resilience of the grid by building on local adaptations and experimenting with new local systems, integrating them into the national system where feasible.
- encourage private sector collaboration with local authorities, institutions, and communities to replicate and expand these systems.

WEAKER CENTRAL CAPACITY AND LIMITED VESTED INTERESTS

If the political elite lacks the authority or capacity to manage the electricity sector, donors should explore opportunities to work at the central and local levels concurrently. Donor support at the local level will have greater impact during this window of opportunity. They should:

- bolster the government's ability to govern the sector and absorb aid, including by:
  - providing technical support to compensate for the loss of human capital in state utilities;
  - assisting in prioritizing between the competing needs in the sector; and
  - providing financial support for discrete interventions to boost electricity provision in the most cost-effective ways possible, such as repairing sections of transmission lines.
- identify local adaptations that provide electricity and assess the factors that contributed to the success of these islands of resilience, including by:
  - testing the viability of integrating renewable technologies into local adaptations that rely on diesel; and
  - experimenting with different models of decentralized electricity provision that integrate renewables.
- build on local islands of resilience by working directly with local authorities and communities, including by:
  - spreading awareness of these successful initiatives nationally and

with potential private sector investors.

- releasing feasibility studies and business models to ensure that others can replicate successful projects.
- de-risking investments, providing guarantees, and working to unlock climate financing for these initiatives.

STRONGER CENTRAL CAPACITY AND ENTRENCHED VESTED INTERESTS

If the political elite has entrenched vested interests in the status quo but central authorities have the capacity to continue to finance the electricity sector, then donor interventions are likely to have limited impact. MNCs may also profit from the status quo, work to limit competition for major contracts, and frustrate efforts to transition away from hydrocarbon-based electricity generation. Hydrocarbon reserves may allow the government to continue to finance electricity subsidies and resist efforts to make the electricity sector more efficient despite chronic losses. If the social contract leads citizens to believe that their government has a duty to provide cheap electricity, then it will be harder for donors to convince them about the benefits of alternative systems. Donors should:

- insist on aid conditionality for discrete reforms, such the establishment of a legal framework for private investment in renewable energy.
- fund awareness campaigns about the benefits of alternative systems and support high-visibility pilot projects.
- lead by example by mainstreaming energy efficiency and renewable technologies in their aid programs.

WEAKER CENTRAL CAPACITY AND ENTRENCHED VESTED INTERESTS

In situations of weak central capacity and entrenched vested interests, donors have few good options to work at the central level. Donors should:

- avoid supporting temporary fixes in the electricity sector that create new streams of income for corrupt actors that could become permanent.
- raise awareness of islands of resilience that demonstrate the potential of alternatives systems of electricity provision.

ELECTRICITY AND PEACE

Electricity is the foundation of any effective state. But electricity is also an underappreciated tool for limiting conflict and maintaining peaceful societies. It can reduce the drivers of conflict and advance the foundations of sustainable peace. Providing power more consistently diminishes intercommunal tensions, reduces displacement, and limits opportunities for malign actors to profit from the plight of civilians.

The reliable and affordable provision of electricity creates virtuous circles that bring far-reaching and transformational benefits in conflict-affected environments. Renewable technologies facilitate more resilient systems of electricity provision, bolstering the restoration of essential services and livelihoods. Even in the most challenging environments, they can fuel local economic development, establish the foundations of better governance, and set societies on a pathway of greater environmental sustainability.

In 2011, Al-Qaeda in the Arabian Peninsula (AQAP) faced little resistance as it seized territory across Abyan province in southern Yemen. Part of its popularity stemmed from its ability to capitalize on local discontent with the government and provide basic services to a higher standard than the government, including electricity.[269] Although U.S.- and Emirati-backed forces conducted repeated campaigns to expel them from the province, services did not improve, and AQAP kept returning.

In one town in Abyan's Serar district, power was only available at night. Schools could not print readings or exam papers for their students, fans did not work in healthcare centers, and food spoiled in markets because of a lack of refrigeration. The lack of fuel and diesel and high maintenance costs meant that residents of the town were unable to turn to private generators.[270]

"People in nearby districts had success with solar energy projects," Mansour Mohammed, a resident of the town said. "That motivated us to find alternative energy solutions and establish a solar energy system for ourselves." In 2019, European donors supported the installation of a solar-powered micro-grid and trained Mansour and nine other men to manage it. It has provided cheaper, near continuous, and cleaner electricity to homes, schools, clinics, and local businesses. Schools can now operate in the day, business is thriving in the local market, and young people can use their phones for leisure and education.[271] After years of conflict, neglect, and hardship, electricity is powering recovery.

ABOUT THE AUTHORS

WILL TODMAN

is a fellow in the Middle East Program at CSIS. Since joining CSIS in 2016, his research has focused on aid, sustainability, and displacement in the Middle East, with an emphasis on the Levant. He has conducted field research in nine countries across the Middle East and North Africa, and his analysis has been published by peer-reviewed journals, think tanks, and major publications, including the Washington Post. Will has briefed officials from various U.S. government departments and agencies, the UN Security Council, and foreign governments. He has also commented in print and on live television to various outlets, including the BBC, CBS, and CNN. Will is also a 2022–23 Penn Kemble Fellow at the National Endowment for Democracy, a fellow at the Centre for Syrian Studies at St. Andrews University, and a former Global Diversity Fellow at the Atlantic Council. Will previously lived in Beirut, where he worked at the British embassy and for the office of the UN special envoy to Syria. He cofounded KAMA DC, a nonprofit that works with refugees and immigrants, and led the organization for seven years. Will holds a BA in Arabic and modern Hebrew from Oxford University and an MA in Arab studies with a certificate in refugee and humanitarian emergencies from Georgetown University, where he studied Persian intensively.

LUBNA YOUSEF

is a research associate for the Middle East Program at CSIS. Prior to joining CSIS, she served as the disaster response and relief partnerships lead on Airbnb's humanitarian team (now Airbnb.org) and was their resident Atlas Corps fellow before later moving on to be a strategist and manager on Airbnb's Olympic and Paralympic refugee team program. Before her time with Airbnb, Lubna worked on programming and evaluation for projects on women's political participation in local governance in Libya, migration trends in the Mediterranean, and anti-human trafficking measures and associated human rights abuses. She holds a MSc in international politics from the School of Oriental and African Studies (SOAS) and an MA in conflict resolution and coexistence from the Heller School for Social Policy and Management. Her research interests include identity and the politics of memory, gender studies, women in security, post-colonial thought, and the responsibility to protect in humanitarian crises and conflict.

ENDNOTES

1 "أهالي الغوطة الشرقية يحولون الدراجة الهوائية إلى مولدة كهربائية - أخبار الآن" [The people of Eastern Ghouta turn bikes into electricity generators], YouTube video, posted by Al-Aan TV, June 1, 2014, 2:55, https://www.youtube.com/watch?v=sWuqFt9xNRo.

2 Ahmad al-Dimashqi, "Do-it-yourself alternative energy in besieged al-Ghouta," The New Humanitarian, *Syria Deeply,* October 20, 2015, https://deeply.thenewhumanitarian.org/syria/articles/2015/10/20/do-it-yourself-alternative-energy-in-besieged-al-ghouta.

3 "عربة طاقة متنقلة تُوفّر المياه لمدارس الغوطة" [A mobile energy cart that supplies water to schools in Ghouta], Enab Baladi, June 4, 2017, https://www.enabbaladi.net/archives/153858.

4 The terms "donor" and "international donor" are used in this report to refer to governments and institutions which provide humanitarian and development aid and financing to developing countries. This group includes donor governments (particularly North American, European, Arab Gulf, and East Asian states) and international financial institutions (including the Arab Fund for Economic and Social Development, the European Bank for Reconstruction and Development, and the World Bank Group) as well as their implementing partners, including UN organizations and nongovernmental organizations (NGOs).

5 Jihad Azour, Franck Bousquet, and Abebe Aemro Selassie, "Countries hurt by war and fragility need strong global partnerships, resources," International Monetary Fund, December 22, 2022, https://www.imf.org/en/Blogs/Articles/2022/12/21/countries-hurt-by-war-and-fragility-need-strong-global-partnerships-resources.

6 Kimberly Flowers, "Saving lives in a time of crisis: Why the global humanitarian system matters," (public event, CSIS, Washington, DC, February 5, 2019), https://www.csis.org/analysis/saving-lives-time-crisis-why-global-humanitarian-system-matters.

7 In Iraq alone, international donors spent more than $5 billion on electricity infrastructure in the decade after the 2003 U.S.-led invasion.

8 Ted Mann, "GE seeks power sales in Iraq, but report spotlights corruption concerns," Wall Street Journal, November 19, 2022, https://www.wsj.com/articles/ge-seeks-power-sales-in-iraq-but-report-spotlights-corruption-concerns-1542553210.

9 "GE, Turkish company sign deal to support Yemen's electricity infrastructure," *Hurriyet Daily News,* February 14, 2017, https://www.hurriyetdailynews.com/ge-turkish-company-sign-deal-to-support-yemens-electricity-infrastructure-109740; and "Yemen government chooses Siemens Energy to support effort to build country's infrastructure," Power Systems Technology, July 11, 2022, https://www.transformer-technology.com/pst/3437-yemen-government-chooses-siemens-energy-to-support-effort-to-build-country-s-infrastructure-power-systems-technology-news.html.

10 Najia al-Houssari "Lebanon crippled by electricity, water outages," *Arab News*, May 24, 2022, https://www.arabnews.com/node/2088836/middle-east.

11 Neighborhood generator owners operate systems of varying sizes in Lebanon and Iraq. Some have small generators for apartment complexes, but others run shipping container-sized generators that provide subscription services to buildings in entire neighborhoods.

12 Joseph Majkut and Allegra Dawes, "Responding to Russian attacks on Ukraine's power sector," CSIS, *Commentary,* November 8, 2022, https://www.csis.org/analysis/responding-russian-attacks-ukraines-power-sector.

13 International Renewable Energy Agency (IRENA), *Renewable Power Generation Costs in 2020* (Abu Dhabi: June 2021), https://www.irena.org/publications/2021/Jun/Renewable-Power-Costs-in-2020.

14 Hisham Zerriffi, Hadi Dowlatabadi, and Neil Strachan, "Electricity and Conflict: Advantages of a distributed system," *The Electricity Journal* 15, no. 1 (January/February 2002): 55–65, doi:10.1016/S1040-6190(01)00262-7.

15 Sludge-to-energy plants advance a circular economy and have been adopted in developing states. See Vittal Boggaram and Sahana Goswami, "From waste to watts: How sewage could help fix India's water, energy, and sanitation woes," World Resources Institute, March 22, 2017, https://www.wri.org/insights/waste-watts-how-sewage-could-help-fix-indias-water-energy-and-sanitation-woes.

16 As discussed in the Yemen chapter, the UNDP program to support Iman al-Hamali's micro-grid fueled economic recovery, job creation, and contributed to changing gender norms.

17 Layal Shakir, "ISIS claims attacks on 68 electricity towers in Iraq," Rudaw, July 9, 2021, https://www.rudaw.net/english/middleeast/iraq/09072021.

18 Adnan Abu Zeed, "Electrical towers again become targets in Iraq," Al-Monitor, August 18, 2021, https://www.al-monitor.com/originals/2021/08/electrical-towers-again-become-targets-iraq.

19 Author's interview with owner of solar company in Baghdad, Iraq, June 5, 2022.

20 Iraq spends $6.5 million per day, or $2.4 billion per year, on energy subsidies, and Iraqis pay an estimated 10 percent of the kWh cost of electricity. Author's interview with Western diplomats, Baghdad, June 6, 2022.

21 In October 1991, following the Gulf War, UNICEF warned that "the lack of electrical power has eliminated wastewater treatment in Baghdad and southern Iraq and raw sewage is being discharged into waterways." International Study Team, *Health and welfare in Iraq after the Gulf crisis: An in-depth assessment* (New York: UNICEF, October 1991), 7, https://reliefweb.int/sites/reliefweb.int/files/resources/Health_and_Welfare_in_Iraq_after_the_Gulf_Crisis_1991.pdf.

22 Stuart W. Bowen, Jr., *Learning from Iraq: A Final Report from the Special Inspector General for Iraq Reconstruction* (Washington, DC: SIGIR, 2013), 75–76, https://apps.dtic.mil/sti/citations/ADA587236.

23 John Chilcot, *The Report of the Iraq Inquiry*, vol. 9 (London: July 2016), 553, https://webarchive.nationalarchives.gov.uk/ukgwa/20171123122743/http://www.iraqinquiry.org.uk/the-report/.

24 Hideki Matsunaga, *The Reconstruction of Iraq after 2003: Learning from Its Successes and Failures* (Washington, DC: World Bank, 2019), 7, https://openknowledge.worldbank.org/handle/10986/31709.

25 Bowen, Jr., *Learning from Iraq*, 41; and Joseph T. McDermott and Glenn D. Furbush, *Challenges Faced in Carrying Out Iraq Relief and Reconstruction Fund Activities* (Washington, DC: SIGIR, January 2006), iii, https://apps.dtic.mil/sti/citations/ADA517132.

26 Stuart W. Bowen, Jr., and William L. Nash, *Iraq Reconstruction: Lessons in Contracting and Procurement* (Washington, DC: SIGIR, 2006), 42, 46, https://apps.dtic.mil/sti/citations/ADA488742.

27 SIGIR, *Quarterly Reports to the United States Congress* (Washington, DC: October 2009), 64–65, https://cybercemetery.unt.edu/archive/sigir/20131001092911/http://www.sigir.mil/files/quarterlyreports/October2009/Report_-_October_2009.pdf#view=fit; and SIGIR, *Quarterly Report and Semiannual Report to the United States Congress* (Washington, DC: January 2012), 74, https://cybercemetery.unt.edu/archive/sigir/20131001093128/http://www.sigir.mil/files/quarterlyreports/January2012/Report_-_January_2012.pdf#view=fit.

28 Michael Gordon and Isabel Coles, "Defeat of ISIS in Iraq caused $45.7 billion in damage to infrastructure, study finds," *Wall Street Journal*, February 11, 2018, https://www.wsj.com/articles/defeat-of-isis-in-iraq-caused-45-7-billion-in-damage-to-infrastructure-study-finds-1518389411.

29 Author's remote interview with UN officials in Baghdad, May 16, 2022.

30 Author's remote interview with Musab Alkateeb, former CEO of Siemens Iraq, May 17, 2022.

31 Benoit Faucon and Ghassan Adnan, "Iraqi lawmakers call for probe into GE, Siemens electricity contracts," Wall Street Journal, August 20, 2021, https://www.wsj.com/articles/iraqi-lawmakers-call-for-probe-into-ge-siemens-electricity-contracts-11629455913.

32 "العراق.. تحقيق برلماني يكشف إنفاق 81 مليار دولار على الكهرباء منذ 2005" [Iraq… parliamentary investigation reveals $81 billion spent on electricity since 2005], Al-Watan News, December 7, 2020, https://bit.ly/3hcjMcQ.

33 Author's remote interview with Ali al-Saffar, May 11, 2022.

34 World Bank, *Iraq Country Climate and Development Report* (Washington, DC: November 2022), xiii, https://openknowledge.worldbank.org/handle/10986/38250.

35 Harry Istepanian, "Iraq's economic White Paper misses a key issue for the energy sector," Atlantic Council, October 29, 2020, https://www.atlanticcouncil.org/blogs/menasource/iraqs-economic-white-paper-misses-a-key-issue-for-the-energy-sector/.

36 Author's interview with Western diplomats, Baghdad, June 6, 2022.

37 Author's remote interview with H.E. Luay al-Khatteeb, former minister of electricity, June 27, 2022.

38 International Energy Agency (IEA), *Iraq's Energy Sector: A Roadmap to a Brighter Future* (Paris: April 2019), 18, https://iea.blob.core.windows.net/assets/fb1f67b9-3515-4b5a-bb40-06ca0b83ef70/Iraq_Energy_Outlook.pdf.

39 Iraq has the fifth-highest losses from transmission and distribution in the world, based on 2014 World Bank data. "Electric power transmission and distribution losses (% of output)," World Bank, 2018, https://data.worldbank.org/indicator/EG.ELC.LOSS.ZS?most_recent_value_desc=true.

40 Author's interview with Iraqi UN official, Baghdad, June 6, 2022.

41 Author's remote interview with Musab Alkateeb, May 17, 2022.

42 Author's interview with Dr. Ali Allawi, then-deputy prime minister and minister of finance, Baghdad, June 5, 2022.

43 Ali Allawi and Fatih Birol, "Without help for oil-producing countries, net zero by 2050 is a distant dream," *The Guardian*, September 1, 2021, https://www.theguardian.com/commentisfree/2021/sep/01/oil-producing-countries-net-zero-2050-iraq.

44 Author's remote interview with IOM officials, May 16, 2022.

45 Author's remote interview with European diplomat in Baghdad, July 5, 2022.

46 Author's remote interview with Marsin al-Shammary, April 25, 2022; and author's remote interview with European diplomat in Baghdad, July 5, 2022.

47 International Energy Agency, *Sustainable Recovery* (Paris: IEA, June 2020), 10, https://iea.blob.core.windows.net/assets/c3de5e13-26e8-4e52-8a67-b97aba17f0a2/Sustainable_Recovery.pdf.

48 World Bank, *Iraq Country Climate and Development Report*, 24.

49 Ibid., 25.

50 Saleem Salman et al., "Long-term trends in daily temperature extremes in Iraq," *Atmospheric Research* 198 (December 2017), 97–107, https://www.sciencedirect.com/science/article/pii/S0169809517303678?via%3Dihub.

51 Iraq was responsible for 0.5 percent of global CO_2 emissions in 2021. Hannah Ritchie and Max Roser, "Iraq: CO_2 Country Profile," Our World in Data, 2020, https://ourworldindata.org/co2/country/iraq.

52 Author's remote interview with Ambassador Fareed Yasseen, June 7, 2022.

53 Author's interview with HE Ali Allawi, then deputy prime minister and minister of finance, Baghdad, June 5, 2022.

54 The government then planned to expand on this project by adding 1 GW tenders each subsequent year. Author's remote interview with H.E. Luay al-Khatteeb, former minister of electricity, June 27, 2022.

55 "IEA commends Iraq's plans to reform its electricity sector," IEA, September 17, 2019, https://www.iea.org/news/iea-commends-iraqs-plans-to-reform-its-electricity-sector.

56 Author's interview with Saleem Abdullah, CEO of Infinity, Erbil, June 7, 2022.

57 Author's remote interview with UN officials in Iraq, June 1, 2022.

58 Author's interview with the founders of Mosul Solar, Mosul, June 8, 2022; and author's interview with owner of small solar company in Baghdad, June 4, 2022.

59 The program provides individuals up to 18 million IQD ($12,300), medium enterprises up to 206 million IQD ($140,000), and housing complexes up to 1 billion IQD ($680,000). "ضوابط تمويل منظومات توليد الكهرباء من الطاقة المتجددة" [Regulations for financing electricity generation systems from renewable energy], Central Bank of Iraq, n.d., https://cbi.iq/static/uploads/up/file-164130485743553.pdf.

60 Author's interview with Eng. Suha al-Kifae, manager of International Islamic Bank, Baghdad, June 7, 2022.

61 Author's interview with owner of solar company, Baghdad, June 5, 2022; and author's interview with owner of solar company, Mosul, June 8, 2022.

62 Author's interview with owner of solar company, Mosul, June 8, 2022.

63 Author's interview with Western diplomats in Baghdad, June 7, 2022.

64 Author's remote interview with Luay al-Khatteeb, former minister of electricity, June 27, 2022.

65 Author's remote interview with European diplomat in Baghdad, July 5, 2022.

66 Three ministries work directly on the electricity file—the ministries of electricity, oil, and industry—but several other Iraqi institutions and actors wield outsized influence. The prime minister's office, the ministry of finance, the central bank, the parliamentary energy committee, and political parties all intervene in and shape the sector.

67 Author's interview with owner of solar business, Baghdad, June 4, 2022.

68 Author's remote interview with Musab Alkateeb, May 17, 2022.

69 Ibid.

70 Ibid.

71 "GE settles SEC charges on Iraq kickback scheme," Reuters, July 27, 2010, https://www.reuters.com/article/us-ge/ge-settles-sec-charges-on-iraq-kickback-scheme-idUKTRE66M3O820100727; and "Siemens AG and three subsidiaries plead guilty to Foreign Corrupt Practice Act violations and agree to pay $450 million in combined criminal fines," U.S. Department of Justice, December 15, 2008, https://www.justice.gov/archive/opa/pr/2008/December/08-crm-1105.html.

72 Author's interview with UN official, Baghdad, June 6, 2022.

73 Prices of electricity vary by region, ranging from an estimated 5,000 IQD ($3.43) to 25,000 IQD ($17.14) per amp depending on the region.

74 Author's interview with academic at Mosul University, June 8, 2022.

75 Samya Kullab, "Shadow contracts, corruption keep the lights out in Iraq," Associated Press, September 27, 2021, https://apnews.com/article/business-middle-east-elections-iraq-baghdad-177d3284c-87d892ac4f9f56140f13331.

76 "Iraq: Executive Summary," EIA, updated September 28, 2022, https://www.eia.gov/international/analysis/country/IRQ.

77 Zeinab Shuker, "Gas flaring in Iraq: Structural issues, geopolitical players, and policy implications," Emirates Policy Center, April 11, 2022, https://epc.ae/en/details/featured/gas-flaring-in-iraq-structural-issues-geopolitical-players-and-policy-implications.

78 World Bank, *Iraq Country Climate and Development Report;* and Alissa Rubin and Clifford Krauss, "Southern Iraq's toxic twilight: burning gas and poisoning the air," *New York Times,* July 16, 2020, https://www.nytimes.com/2020/07/16/world/middleeast/iraq-gas-flaring-cancer-environment.html.

79 Author's interview with UN official, Baghdad, June 5, 2022.

80 One owner of a solar company said his sales increased by 200 percent after receiving a UNDP training course. Author's interview with Amer al-Azaawy, June 5, 2022.

81 Author's remote interview with salesman from Chinese solar company operating in Iraq, June 29, 2022.

82 Author's interview with academic at Mosul University, June 8, 2022.

83 Author's remote interview with UNDP official, June 1, 2022.

84 Author's interview with UN official, May 25, 2022.

85 The investigation found links between the two primary businesses involved in the scheme and Gebran Bassil from the Free Patriotic Movement, Nabih Berri from the Amal Movement, Suleiman Frangieh from the Marada Movement, Samir Geagea from the Lebanese Forces, and Walid Jumblatt from the Progressive Socialist Party. Figures across Lebanon's political and sectarian spectrum appeared complicit. "Lebanon's Electricity: The largest corruption allegations," YouTube video, posted by BBC News, June 29, 2021, 49:57, https://www.youtube.com/watch?v=OC42WeITQJA.

86 Israel launched six attacks against EDL power stations between 1996 and 2006. J. Nucho, *Everyday Sectarianism in Urban Lebanon: Infrastructures, Public Services, And Power* (Princeton, NJ: Princeton University Press, 2017).

87 Marc Ayoub, "كم أنفقت الدولة اللبنانية فعلياً على الكهرباء؟" [How much has the Lebanese state actually spent on electricity?] Al-Sifr, October 27, 2022, https://alsifr.org/electricity-expenditure-lebanon.

88 Abou Jaoude, Hachem El Housseini, and Souraya Machnouk, "In review: Energy regulation in Lebanon," Lexology, June 2, 2022, https://www.lexology.com/library/detail.aspx?g=6b3d28e9-9704-4229-9508-7c5f5f25c33e.

89 There was no audit of EDL between 2010 and 2022. Sunniva Rose, "Lebanon: audit of collapsing state power company paves way for regional power deal," *The National,* March 7, 2022, https://www.thenationalnews.com/mena/2022/03/07/lebanon-audit-of-collapsing-state-power-company-paves-way-for-regional-power-deal/; and Jaoude. El Housseini, and Machnouk, "In review: Energy regulation in Lebanon."

90 CSIS compilation of data on international donor spending in the electricity sector from "Funding," Council for Development and Reconstruction, n.d., https://www.cdr.gov.lb/en-US/Funding.aspx.

91 Christine Sylva Hamieh and Roger Mac Ginty, "A Very Political Reconstruction: Governance and Reconstruction in Lebanon after the 2006 War," *Disasters* 34, no. 1 (2010), 103–23, doi:10.1111/j.1467-

7717.2009.01101.x.

92 Carol Ayat et al., "Keeping the Lights On: A Short-Term Action Plan for Lebanon's Electricity Sector," Issam Fares Institute for Public Policy and International Affairs, Konrad Adenauer Stiftung, and National Resource Governance Institute, March 2021, https://www.aub.edu.lb/ifi/Documents/publications/Other%20Publications/2021-2022/202103_Keeping_the_Lights_on_paper.pdf.

93 Author's interview with UN official in Beirut, May 25, 2022; and Marc Ayoub, "خارطة احتكارات النّفط في لبنان" [Map of the oil monopolies in Lebanon], Legal Agenda, December 8, 2020, https://bit.ly/3FLKV0q.

94 Ayoub, "How much has the Lebanese state actually spent on electricity?"

95 Nada Maucourant Atallah, "Juicy contract, suspicious call for tenders – in the murky waters of Lebanon's floating power plants," L'Orient Today, July 28, 2021, https://today.lorientlejour.com/article/1269444/juicy-contract-suspicious-call-for-tenders-in-the-murky-waters-of-lebanons-floating-power-plants-part-i-of-ii.html.

96 Ali Ahmad, *Distributed Power Generation for Lebanon: Market Assessment and Policy Recommendations* (Washington, DC: The World Bank Group, May 2020), https://openknowledge.worldbank.org/handle/10986/33788.

97 Author's interview with UN official in Beirut, May 25, 2022.

98 EDF estimated 18 percent technical losses and 27 percent non-technical losses in 2021.

99 Sana'a al-Jack, "Lebanon's state electricity company: A pawn for political corruption," *Asharq al-Awsat,* July 23, 2018, https://english.aawsat.com/home/article/1340481/lebanon%E2%80%99s-state-electricity-company-pawn-political-corruption.

100 Author's interview with Lebanese electricity sector official, Beirut, May 27, 2022.

101 World Bank Group, *International Bank for Reconstruction and Development, International Finance Corporation, and Multilateral Investment Guarantee Agency Country Partnership Framework for the Lebanese Republic for the period FY17-FY22* (Washington, DC: World Bank Group, June 2016), 21, https://documents1.worldbank.org/curated/en/111451467996685776/pdf/94768-CAS-P151022-R2016-0126-OUO-9-Box396270B.pdf.

102 The Economic Conference for Development through Reforms with the Private Sector (CEDRE) offered Lebanon $11 billion in loans and grants in exchange for "essential" reforms in the electricity sector, including "an ambitious tariff reform alongside increased power generation." "CEDRE Joint Statement," French Ministry of European and Foreign Affairs, April 6, 2018, https://www.diplomatie.gouv.fr/IMG/pdf/cedre_statement-en-_final_ang_cle8179fb.pdf.

103 "Lebanon central bank effectively lifts fuel subsidies," Reuters, August 11, 2021, https://www.reuters.com/world/middle-east/lebanese-cbank-says-can-no-longer-subsidise-fuel-report-2021-08-11/; and "Lebanon raises cost of electricity for first time since 1990s," Reuters, November 1, 2022, https://www.reuters.com/world/middle-east/lebanon-raises-cost-electricity-first-time-since-1990s-spokesperson-2022-11-01/.

104 Author's interview World Bank Group official, Lebanon, May 27, 2022.

105 Author's remote interview with Zaccariah Nasreddine, mayor of al-Ain, Lebanon, February 2, 2023; and author's interview with Omar Jheir, owner of SIP, Beirut, May 27, 2022.

106 Sunniva Rose, "Lebanon swaps $200m in fuel with Iraq for in-kind services," *The National,* April 5, 2021, https://www.thenationalnews.com/mena/lebanon/lebanon-swaps-200m-in-fuel-with-iraq-for-in-kind-services-1.1196641.

107 Will Todman, "The Politics of Lebanon's Gas Deal with Egypt and Syria," CSIS, *Critical Questions,* June

23, 2022, https://www.csis.org/analysis/politics-lebanons-gas-deal-egypt-and-syria.

108 Lebanon has plans for a 67.2 MW onshore wind farm in northern Lebanon known as Hawa Akkar, but it is in the permitting phase. The government also issued licenses for 11 projects that total 165 MW of solar capacity in 2022, but progress on these projects remains unclear while Lebanon's economic collapse continues.

109 Author's remote interview with member of the 3RF consultative group for the electricity sector, April 28, 2022.

110 Author's interview with UN official, Lebanon, May 25, 2022.

111 Author's interview with UN official, Lebanon, May 26, 2022.

112 Timour Azhari and Maya Gebeily, "Public sector paralysed as Lebanon lurches towards 'failed state'," Reuters, August 18, 2022, https://www.reuters.com/world/middle-east/public-sector-paralysed-lebanon-lurches-towards-failed-state-2022-08-18/.

113 Author's interview with EDL official, Lebanon, May 26, 2022.

114 Author's interview with UN official, Lebanon, May 25, 2022.

115 Author's interview with Pierre Khoury, Lebanese Center for Energy Conservation, Ministry of Energy and Water Resources, Beirut, May 27, 2022.

116 Author's interview with Pierre Khoury, Lebanese Center for Energy Conservation, Ministry of Energy and Water Resources, Beirut, May 27, 2022.

117 Author's interview with Zaccariah Nasreddine, mayor of al-Ain, Lebanon, May 23, 2022.

118 Author's interview with EDL official, Lebanon, May 26, 2022.

119 Author's interview with Lebanese employee in Western embassy, Lebanon, May 24, 2022.

120 Author's interview with INGO official, Lebanon, May 24, 2022.

121 Banque de l'Habitat and LCEC, "List of qualified solar PV companies – December 2022," Lebanese Center for Energy Conservation, December 2022, https://lcec.org.lb/sites/default/files/2022-12/BDH_List%20of%20Qualified%20Solar%20PV%20Companies_20221206.pdf.

122 Author's remote interview with Jessica Obeid, energy consultant, May 4, 2022.

123 Author's interview with UN official, Lebanon, May 25, 2022.

124 Alix Chaplain, "Strategies of power and the emergence of hybrid mini-grids in Lebanon," Jadaliyya, March 8, 2022, https://www.jadaliyya.com/Details/43932.

125 Author's interview with EDL official, Lebanon, May 26, 2022.

126 Author's remote interview with Rony Karam, Lebanese Foundation for Renewable Energy, May 6, 2022.

127 "Lebanon: UN expert warns of 'failing State' amid widespread poverty," United Nations Office of the High Commissioner for Human Rights, May 11, 2022, https://www.ohchr.org/en/press-releases/2022/05/lebanon-un-expert-warns-failing-state-amid-widespread-poverty; and "Lebanon's Crisis: Great Denial in the Deliberate Depression," World Bank, January 25, 2022, https://www.worldbank.org/en/news/press-release/2022/01/24/lebanon-s-crisis-great-denial-in-the-deliberate-depression.

128 Author's interview with European donor official, Beirut, May 25, 2022.

129 Author's interview with UN officials, Beirut, May 26, 2022.

130 Author's interviews with UN officials, Lebanon, May 23–27, 2022.

131 The Lebanon Reform, Recovery, and Reconstruction Framework (3RF) is a joint initiative of the European Union, United Nations, and World Bank Group. Author's remote interview with member of the 3RF consultative group for the electricity sector, April 28, 2022.

132 Author's remote interview with UN official, March 14, 2022.

133 USAID awarded the Innovation for Affordable and Renewable Energy for All (INARA) contract to IMC Worldwide (now DT Global) in September 2021.

134 Author's interview with Nadia Alami and Christina Abi Haidar of INARA, Lebanon, May 26, 2022.

135 "INARA Launch Event Rechmaya," YouTube video, posted by INARA Lebanon, October 6, 2022, 1:30, https://www.youtube.com/watch?v=iCM7VDmxMeU.

136 INARA Lebanon, "INARA Solar Intervention," YouTube video, posted by INARA Lebanon, September 9, 2022, 2:43, https://www.youtube.com/watch?v=syIaELUjSPE.

137 Author's interviews with representatives from four European and Asian embassies in Beirut, May 23–26, 2022.

138 Author's interview with Nadia Alami and Christina Abi Haidar of INARA, Lebanon, May 26, 2022.

139 For more information about the projects, see "Regional initiative to promote small-scale renewable energy applications in rural areas of the Arab region," UNESCWA, n.d., https://www.unescwa.org/regend.

140 Author's interview with INGO officials, Lebanon, May 24, 2022.

141 Author's interview with Western diplomat, Lebanon, May 24, 2022.

142 Author's interview with Nadia Alami and Christina Abi Haidar of INARA, Lebanon, May 26, 2022.

143 Miriam Bala'a, "ميقاتي ينبّه فيّاض إلى استحالة التعديل... فهل تمرّ 'الهيئة الناظمة للكهرباء'؟!" [Mikati warns Fayyad that amendments are impossible… will the 'Electricity Regulatory Authority' pass?]. Al-Markaziya, December 13, 2022, https://bit.ly/3YtG7E1.

144 Rédaction Africanews, "Libyans endure longer, frequent power-cuts," African News, July 14, 2022, https://www.africanews.com/2022/07/14/libyans-endure-longer-frequent-power-cuts/.

145 Mohamed Elmagbri et al., *Challenges and Steps Forward for Public Services Reform in Libya* (Libya: Friedrich-Ebert-Stiftung, March 2022), 19, https://library.fes.de/pdf-files/bueros/libyen/19556.pdf.

146 Author's remote interview with Dr. Medhat Elgdhamsi, private sector adviser and former World Bank consultant, October 9, 2022; and author's remote interview with former UNSMIL adviser, October 20, 2022.

147 Author's remote interview with Dr. Medhat Elgdhamsi, private sector adviser and former World Bank consultant, October 9, 2022; and author's remote interview with former UNSMIL adviser, October 20, 2022.

148 World Bank Group, *Task A: sector performance and structural sector reform: Deliverable 5: Final report* (Washington, DC: 2017), 28, http://documents.worldbank.org/curated/en/616071527050024484/Task-A-sector-performance-and-structural-sector-reform-deliverable-five-final-report.

149 "Electricity Prices for Households," Global Petrol Prices, March 2022, https://www.globalpetrolprices.com/electricity_prices/.

150 Author's remote interview with Emadeddin Badi, Libyan political analyst, September 21, 2022; author's interview with Ahmed Shalghoum, Libyan political analyst, September 26, 2022; and author's

remote interview with Western donor official working on Libya, September 21, 2022.

151 El-Kul, Facebook, June 20, 2019, https://www.facebook.com/elkul.libya/posts/2261527010635170/.

152 Saddek Elkaber, "Saddek Elkaber: a lesson from Libya's central bank," The Banker, October 1, 2019, https://www.thebanker.com/World/Africa/Libya/Saddek-Elkaber-a-lesson-from-Libya-s-central-bank.

153 Mattisan Rowan, "Libya Timeline: Since Qaddafi's Ouster," United States Institute of Peace, July 1, 2019, https://www.usip.org/libya-timeline-qaddafis-ouster.

154 "2020 Investment Climate Statements: Libya," U.S. Department of State, 2020, https://www.state.gov/reports/2020-investment-climate-statements/libya/.

155 World Bank Group, *Libya Economic Monitor* (Washington, DC: 2021), 3, https://thedocs.worldbank.org/en/doc/3d3cd163628175d3add84db3c707eaa5-0280012021/original/ENG-Libya-Economic-Monitor.pdf.

156 MEE and agencies, "Four foreign engineers kidnapped in Libya," Middle East Eye, November 3, 2017, https://www.middleeasteye.net/fr/news/four-foreign-engineers-kidnapped-libya-39688726.

157 Mohamed Almaktar et al., "Revitalizing operational reliability of the electrical energy system in Libya: Feasibility analysis of solar generation in local communities," *Journal of Cleaner Production* (January 2021), 3, doi:10.1016/j.jclepro.2020.123647; and "Libyan Electricity Sector Stabilization and Transition Support (LESST), MPTF Office Generic Annual Programme 1 Narrative Progress Report," UNDP and UNEF, 2020, 2, https://mptf.undp.org/sites/default/files/documents/40000/38543.

158 Libyan Audit Bureau, "التقرير السنوي لديوان المحاسبة الليبي 2021م" [Libyan Audit Bureau Report 2021], (Tripoli: 2021), 397–422, https://www.audit.gov.ly/ar/reports/.

159 Sami Zaptia, "Audit Bureau refers file of causes of power cuts to Attorney General, recommends travel ban for GECOL officials," *Libyan Herald*, August 30, 2020, https://www.libyaherald.com/2020/08/audit-bureau-refers-file-of-causes-of-power-cuts-to-attorney-general-recommends-travel-ban-for-gecol-officials/; and "The Libyan Audit Bureau recommends travel ban for GECOL officials," Tabadul, August 27, 2020, https://tabadul.tv/en/the-libyan-audit-bureau-recommends-travel-ban-for-gecol-officials/.

160 Zaptia, "Audit Bureau refers file of causes of power cuts to Attorney General."

161 "ديوان المحاسبة: تعاقدات الشركة العامة للكهرباء تجاوزت 16 مليار دينار خلال 2021" [Audit Bureau: Contracts of the General Electricity Company exceeded 16 billion dinars during 2021], *Alwasat,* 2022, https://alwasat.ly/news/libya/372655

162 Elmagbri et al., *Challenges and Steps Forward for Public Services Reform in Libya.*

163 "العبدلي يوضح سبب انهيار الشبكة العامة للكهرباء" [Al-Abdali explains the cause of the collapse of the public electricity network], Libyan News Agency, June 28, 2021, http://www.lananews.com/ar/?p=238350; El-Kul, Facebook post, June 20, 2019, https://www.facebook.com/elkul.libya/posts/2261527010635170/; and Muhammad Artima, "الكهرباء في ليبيا.. جهود حثيثة لاحتواء الأزمة" [Electricity in Libya.. Unremitting Efforts to Contain the Crisis (Interview)], AA, January 2, 2021, https://bit.ly/3Gsitj1.

164 Author's remote interview with Emadeddin Badi, Libyan political analyst, September 21, 2022; author's remote interview with international development officer from Libya, September 23, 2022; author's remote interview with Ahmed Shalghoum, Libyan political analyst, September 26, 2022; author's remote interview with Western donor's implementing partner working in Libya, Libya Office, September 27, 2022; interview with Dr. Medhat Elgdhamsi, private sector adviser and former World Bank consultant, October 9, 2022; and interview with Matthew Brubacher, economic and energy adviser, October 2022.

165 Kaouther Abderrahim and Yasmine Eita, *Libya Country Brief 2021–2022* (Abidjan, Côte d'Ivoire: African Development Bank, 2021), 8, https://www.afdb.org/en/documents/libya-country-brief-2021-2022.

166 "التقرير السنوي لديوان المحاسبة الليبي 2021م" [Libyan Audit Bureau, Annual Libyan Audit Bureau Report (Tripoli: 2021)], 408, https://bit.ly/3GOOd3i. This conversion is based on the amount of outstanding debt from end consumers described as households, businesses, and public entities as provided by the LAB 2021 report. The number reported in Libyan dinars is 4,368,579,151.000. The conversion to U.S. dollars is based on the exchange rate for the year 2023 as provided by https://www.xe.com/currencyconverter/, a site offered as an external resource by the Internal Revenue Service.

167 "مولدات الكهرباء - ليبيا" [Libya- electricity generators], Facebook post, https://www.facebook.com/groups/540879863267642.

168 It is important to note that waves of conflict tend to impact availability of fuel for generators, pushing consumers to seek black market supplies at double the price. Source: Tom Westcott, "Running on Empty: Oil-rich Libya hit by extreme oil shortages," Middle East Eye, March 24, 2020.

169 "The World Bank in Libya," World Bank Group, October 20, 2022, https://www.worldbank.org/en/country/libya/overview#1.

170 Ahmed Elumami and Ayman Al-Warfali, "Libya's power cuts enrage citizens, spurring protest," Reuters, July 2022, https://www.reuters.com/world/africa/libyas-power-cuts-enrage-citizens-spurring-protest-2022-07-04/.

171 "Top Renewable Energy Projects in Libya," Energy Capital and Power, October 28, 2021, https://energycapitalpower.com/top-renewable-energy-projects-in-libya/.

172 Emiliano Bellini, "Total Energies, Gecol to build 500 MW of solar in Libya," *PV Magazine*, June 17, 2022, https://www.pv-magazine.com/2022/06/17/totalenergies-gecol-to-build-500-mw-of-solar-in-libya/.

173 Author's remote interview with Ahmed Shalghoum, Libyan political analyst, September 26, 2022.

174 Author's remote interview Muhammad Kowash, international development officer in Tripoli, Libya, September 23, 2022.

175 Nadia Benamara, "UNDP solar power project in Libya helps save lives," OPEC Fund for International Development, January 01, 2018, https://opecfund.org/news/undp-solar-power-project-in-libya-helps-save-lives.

176 Author's remote interview with Emadeddin Badi, September 21, 2022; author's remote interview with Muhammad Kowash, September 23, 2022; author's remote interview with Ahmed Shalghoum, September 26, 2022; author's remote interview with Western donor's implementing partner working in Libya, September 27, 2022; author's interview with Dr. Medhat Elgdhamsi, October 9, 2022; and author's remote interview with Matthew Brubacher, October 20, 2022.

177 Author's remote interview with Matthew Brubacher, October 2022.

178 Ibid.

179 Author's remote interview with Emadeddin Badi, September 21, 2022; author's remote interview with Muhammad Kowash, September 23, 2022; author's remote interview with Ahmed Shalghoum, September 26, 2022; author's remote interview with Western donor's implementing partner working in Libya, September 27, 2022; author's interview with Dr. Medhat Elgdhamsi, October 9, 2022; and author's remote interview with Matthew Brubacher, October 20, 2022.

180 Author's remote interview with Matthew Brubacher, October 2022.

181 "Libya Public Financial Management (LPFM) program," USAID, August 12, 2022, https://www.usaid.gov/libya/fact-sheets/libya-public-financial-management-lpfm.

182 Author's remote interview with Western donor official working on Libya, September 21, 2022; author's remote interview with Western donor's implementing partner working in Libya, September 27, 2022;

and author's remote interview with development worker, September 23, 2022.

183 Author's remote interview with Western donor official working on Libya, September 21, 2022; and author's remote interview with Dr. Medhat Elgdhamsi, October 9, 2022.

184 Author's remote interview with Matthew Brubacher.

185 Al Arabiya News, "Power cut protests hit Libyan cities, showing anger at factional leaders," Al Arabiya, July 1, 2022, https://english.alarabiya.net/News/north-africa/2022/07/01/Power-cut-protests-hit-Libyan-cities-showing-anger-at-factional-leaders.

186 Safa Alharathy, "Dbeibah sacks GECOL management and refers it to investigation," Libya Observer, June 27, 2020, https://libyaobserver.ly/news/dbeibah-sacks-gecol-management-and-refers-it-investigation; and Al Arabiya News, "Power cut protests hit Libyan cities, showing anger at factional leaders."

187 Libyan Express, "GNU: Electricity crisis is caused by a shutdown of oil production and exports," Libya Observer, June 26, 2022, https://www.libyanexpress.com/gnu-libyas-electricity-crisis-is-caused-by-a-shutdown-of-oil-production-and-exports/.

188 Ahmed Alkhamisy, "كهرباء ليبيا تواجه أزمة نقص غاز" [Libya's electricity faces a gas shortage crisis], Alaraby, September 08, 2022, https://bit.ly/3Zra2NM.

189 In 2017, Siemens signed a €700 million ($751 million) contract to improve the generation capacity for GECOL. "Siemens signs contracts with GECOL to boost power generation capacity in Libya by 1.3 GW," Siemens, December 11, 2017, https://press.siemens.com/middleeast/en/pressrelease/siemens-signs-contracts-gecol-boost-power-generation-capacity-libya-13-gw; and Libyan Audit Bureau, *Libyan Audit Bureau Report 2021*, 400.

190 Sami Zaptia, "Audit Bureau rejects overpriced €250 m direct commissioning Siemens maintenance contract as illegal," *Libya Herald*, September 15, 2020, https://www.libyaherald.com/2020/09/audit-bureau-rejects-overpriced-e-250-m-direct-commissioning-siemens-maintenance-contract-as-illegal/.

191 Author's remote interview with political economy analyst, October 2022; and "معلقًا على أزمة الكهرباء.. امغيب: لا استبعد أن تكون هناك صفقة مولدات لعائلة الدبيبات" [Commenting on the electricity crisis .. Maghib: I do not rule out the Dbeibah family has an electricity generators deal], Libya Alhadath, June 27, 2022, https://libyaalhadath.net/?p=103457.

192 Author's remote interview with Emadeddin Badi, September 21, 2022.

193 "Decree No. (33) of 2012 on approving the organizational structure and competencies of the Ministry of Electricity and Renewable Energy and organizing its administrative unit," The Cabinet of Libya, translation provided by DCAF Trust Fund for North America, June 2, 2012, 3, https://s3-eu-west-1.amazonaws.com/public.ldil.dcaf/law/258-Decree%20No.%20(33)%20of%202012_EN.pdf.

194 Author's remote interview with Emadeddin Badi, September 21, 2022.

195 Author's remote interview with Dr. Medhat Elghdamsi, October 9, 2022.

196 CSIS hired a Yemeni consultant to conduct additional interviews in Yemen for this chapter. CSIS has not identified the individual at the consultant's request.

197 "Iman, the solar-powered heroine inspiring change in rural Yemen," UNDP, March 7, 2021, https://www.undp.org/yemen/stories/iman-solar-powered-heroine-inspiring-change-rural-yemen.

198 The date of the outbreak of Yemen's conflict is disputed. The Houthis occupied Sana'a in 2014, and the Saudi-led coalition began its military intervention in 2015.

199 Towfick Sufian, Can Ogutcu, and Matteo Barra, *Energy Investment and Business Climate Report for Observer Countries: The Republic of Yemen* (Brussels: International Energy Charter, November 2016), 18, https://www.energycharter.org/fileadmin/DocumentsMedia/Occasional/Yemen_Investment_Report.pdf.

200 Akram Almohamadi, *Priorities for the Recovery and Reform of the Electricity Sector in Yemen* (Sana'a, Yemen: DeepRoot Consulting, May 2021), 17, https://carpo-bonn.org/wp-content/uploads/2021/05/Rethinking_Yemens_Economy_No8_En.pdf.

201 "National Strategy for Renewable Energy and Energy Efficiency," Ministry of Electricity and Energy, the Republic of Yemen, June 2009, https://www.climate-laws.org/geographies/yemen/policies/national-strategy-for-renewable-energy-and-energy-efficiency.

202 Author's remote interview with Yemeni development expert, November 17, 2022.

203 Author's email correspondence with Helen Lackner, November 10, 2022.

204 "Siemens/Bemco team in front for Marib power station," MEED Middle East Business Intelligence, August 20, 2004, https://www.meed.com/siemensbemco-team-in-front-for-marib-power-station/; and Almohamadi, *Priorities for the Recovery and Reform of the Electricity Sector in Yemen,* 29.

205 Almohamadi, *Priorities for the Recovery and Reform of the Electricity Sector in Yemen,* 29.

206 World Bank, *International Development Association Project Appraisal Document on a Proposed Grand in the Amount of SDR 13 million (US$20 million equivalent) to the Republic of Yemen for the Mocha Wind Park Project* (Washington, DC: World Bank, February 2014), https://documents1.worldbank.org/curated/en/156751468335513164/pdf/PAD6510P146055010Box382145B00OUO090.pdf.

207 This project was funded by the Yemeni government, the World Bank, the Islamic Development Bank, the Agence Française de Développement, the German government, and others. See: World Bank, *Project Appraisal Document on a Proposed Grant in the Amount of SDR 16.8 Million (US$25 Million Equivalent) to the Republic of Yemen for a Rural Energy Access Project* (Washington, DC: World Bank, April 2009), https://documents1.worldbank.org/curated/en/105431468334286440/pdf/481400PAD0P092101Official0Use0Only1.pdf.

208 Ghassan Khaled Ismail al-Akwaa, "Measuring electricity access amidst active conflict: Lessons from Yemen," World Bank Blogs, May 7, 2019, https://blogs.worldbank.org/energy/measuring-electricity-access-amidst-active-conflict-lessons-yemen.

209 In areas further from the most intense fighting, electricity provision is similar to pre-conflict levels. PEC officials in al-Mahra and Hadhramout reported that the conflict has not caused as much damage to the electricity infrastructure in their governorates as in other areas, and daily outages are much shorter. Consultant's interviews, September 15, 2022, and September 26, 2022.

210 Consultant's interview with NGO official in Ta'iz, September 28, 2022.

211 Akram Almohamadi et al., *Improving electricity services in Yemen: priorities and options* (London: International Growth Centre, London School of Economics and Political Science, November 2021), 25, https://www.theigc.org/sites/default/files/2021/11/Improving-electricity-services-in-Yemen_Final-report.pdf .

212 Author's remote interview with Yemeni analyst, November 17, 2022.

213 Mohammad al-Saidi, "Virtue out of necessity: Yemen's lessons on resilience and infrastructure planning," CSIS, *Commentary,* March 25, 2021, https://www.csis.org/analysis/virtue-out-necessity-yemens-lessons-resilience-and-infrastructure-planning.

214 Author's remote interview with Yemeni development expert, November 17, 2022.

215 Author's remote interview with Rafat al-Akhali, November 17, 2022.

216 "Yemen monthly economic update," World Bank Group, March 2020, 7, https://documents1.worldbank.org/curated/en/339571587498517757/pdf/Yemen-Monthly-Economic-Update-March-2020.pdf.

217 Consultant's interview with INGO worker in Yemen, September 29, 2022.

218 Author's remote interview with Rafat al-Akhali, November 17, 2022.

219 Consultant's interview with INGO worker in Yemen, September 18, 2022.

220 Sana'a Center for Strategic Studies, *Beyond the Business as Usual Approach: Combatting Corruption in Yemen* (Sana'a, Yemen: Sana'a Center for Strategic Studies, November 2018), https://sanaacenter.org/files/Rethinking_Yemens_Economy_No4_En.pdf.

221 Consultant's interview with PEC official in Aden, September 18, 2022; and consultant's interview with PEC official in Shabwah, September 21, 2022.

222 Author's email correspondence with Helen Lackner, November 10, 2022.

223 Almohamadi, *Priorities for the Recovery and Reform of the Electricity Sector in Yemen*, 44.

224 The Houthi regulatory authority sets a maximum price per kWh that private generators in areas under their control can charge. In December 2022, they lowered it to 310 riyals. "وزارة الكهرباء تعلن التسعيرة الجديدة للوحدة المباعة للكهرباء" [The Ministry of Electricity announces the new price per unit of electricity], Ministry of Electricity and Energy, December 24, 2022, https://www.moee.gov.ye/news/topic/279.

225 Author's remote interview with IFI official, November 27, 2022.

226 Consultant's interview with INGO worker in Yemen, September 29, 2022.

227 Consultant's interview with MoEE official, September 19, 2022.

228 Consultant's interview with INGO worker in Yemen, September 18, 2022.

229 For a map of projects funded under UNOPS, see "Yemen Emergency Electricity Access Project," United Nations Office for Project Services, accessed November 1, 2022, https://unops-yemen.maps.arcgis.com/apps/dashboards/372187346c1544008bf65e72aaebc154.

230 This view was common across a range of interviewees in different parts of Yemen. Consultant's interview with PEC official in Hadhramout, September 15, 2022; consultant's interview with INGO official, September 18, 2022; consultant's interview with PEC official in Shabwah, September 21, 2022; consultant's interview with INGO official in Marib, September 22, 2022; and consultant's interview with NGO official in Ta'iz, September 28, 2022.

231 Musaed M. Aklan and Helen Lackner, "Solar-powered irrigation in Yemen: Opportunities, challenges, and policies," Sana'a Center for Strategic Studies, April 29, 2021, https://sanaacenter.org/files/Rethinking_Yemens_Economy-policy_brief_22.pdf.

232 Consultant's interview with MoEE official, September 27, 2022.

233 "Saudi Arabia to give Yemeni government $422 mln worth of fuel," Reuters, March 30, 2021, https://www.reuters.com/world/middle-east/saudi-arabia-give-yemeni-government-422-mln-worth-fuel-2021-03-30/.

234 "The Saudi oil derivatives grant," Saudi Development and Reconstruction Program for Yemen, https://saudioilgrant.org/en/province.

235 Author's remote interviews with Yemeni analyst, October 10, 2022; and author's remote interview with Yemeni development expert, November 17, 2022.

236 Author's remote interview with Yemeni development analyst, November 17, 2022.

237 An official working on the project said that UNDP plans to release these studies after a full financial assessment of the various community-level micro- and mini-grid projects has been completed. Author's remote interview with UNDP official in Yemen, February 7, 2023.

238 Miguel Hadchity, "Lebanon's only running power plant will be forcibly out of service as of tomorrow," The 961, August 25, 2022, https://www.the961.com/lebanon-al-zahrani-power-plant-out-of-service/.

239 "UAE signs deal to build $100 million power plant in Yemen: UAE state news agency," Reuters, June 12, 2019, https://www.reuters.com/article/us-emirates-yemen-electricity/uae-signs-deal-to-build-100-million-power-plant-in-yemen-uae-state-news-agency-idUSKCN1TD110.

240 Author's interview with Ammar al-Hayani, owner of al-Taraib Solar, Baghdad, June 5, 2022.

241 Andrew Barnett and Neil McCulloch, "The World Bank discovers power in the power sector," The Policy Practice, *Policy Brief* 14, December 2020, https://www.thepolicypractice.com/sites/default/files/2021-03/PolicyBrief14%20Barnett%20and%20McCulloch%20Policy%20Brief.pdf.

242 Ali Ahmad and Elisabeth Maier, "Why engaging people on energy sector reforms matters in the Middle East and North Africa," World Bank Blogs, December 9, 2020, https://blogs.worldbank.org/arabvoices/why-engaging-people-energy-sector-reforms-matters-middle-east-and-north-africa.

243 Jon Alterman, Natasha Hall, and Will Todman, *Sustainable States: Environment, Governance, and the Future of the Middle East* (Lanham, MD: Rowman & Littlefield, 2021), https://www.csis.org/analysis/sustainable-states-environment-governance-and-future-middle-east.

244 Author's interview with EDL employee, Lebanon, May 26, 2022.

245 See Sophie Bloemeke, "Post-Disaster Recovery Governance, Aid Architecture, and Civil Society Participation: The case of Lebanon's Reform, Recovery and Reconstruction Framework" (master's thesis, American University of Beirut, May 2022), https://scholarworks.aub.edu.lb/bitstream/handle/10938/23465/BloemekeSophie_2022.pdf.

246 Colum Lynch and Amy Mackinnon, "Greed and graft at U.N. climate program," Foreign Policy, August 14, 2019, https://foreignpolicy.com/2019/08/14/greed-and-graft-at-un-climate-program-united-nations-undp-corruption/; and Julian Borger, "UN tribunal finds ethics office failed to protect whistleblower," The Guardian, June 27, 2012, https://www.theguardian.com/world/2012/jun/27/un-tribunal-whistleblower-james-wasserstrom.

247 See Fredrik Galtung and Martin Tisné, "A New Approach to Postwar Reconstruction," *Journal of Democracy* 20, no. 4 (October 2009), doi:10.1353/jod.0.0132; and Christi F. Freeman, "The Failures of Post-Conflict Reconstruction in Sierra Leone and The Threat to Peace," Joan B. Kroc Institute for International Peace Studies, March 2008.

248 For example, see Mounir Mahmalat and Wassim Maktabi, "How do cartels work? Dealmaking at Lebanon's Council for Development and Reconstruction," The Policy Initiative, September 1, 2022, https://www.thepolicyinitiative.org/article/details/194/how-do-cartels-work-dealmaking-at-lebanon%E2%80%99s-council-for-development-and-reconstruction.

249 Galtung and Tisné, "A New Approach to Postwar Reconstruction."

250 Abhijit Banerjee and Esther Duflo, *Poor Economics: A Radical Rethinking of the Way to Fight Global Poverty* (New York: PublicAffairs, 2011), 265.

251 For more on the idea of second-best but politically feasible approaches to electricity sector reform and an examination of EDZ, see Ali Ahmad et al., "From dysfunctional to functional corruption: the politics of decentralized electricity provision in Lebanon," *Energy Research and Social Science* 86 (April 2022), doi:10.1016/j.erss.2021.102399.

252 Nieves Zuniga, "The impact of 'islands of integrity'," Anti-Corruption Resource Center, 2018, 2, https://www.u4.no/publications/the-impact-of-islands-of-integrity.pdf.

253 Melani Cammett, "Positive deviance cases: Their value for development research, policy, and practice," in Jennifer Widner, Michael Woolcock, and Daniel Ortega Nieto, eds., *The Case for Case Studies: Methods*

and Applications in International Development (Cambridge, UK: Cambridge University Press, 2022).

254 Victoria Konovalenko Slettli and Arvind Singhal, "Identification and Amplification of Tacit Knowledge: the Positive Deviance Approach as Knowledge Management Praxis," *Electronic Journal of Knowledge Management* 15, no. 1 (May 2017), https://academic-publishing.org/index.php/ejkm/article/view/1093.

255 David Patel, Valerie Bunce, and Sharon Wolchik, "Diffusion and demonstration" in Marc Lynch, ed., *The Arab Uprisings Explained: New Contentious Politics in the Middle East* (New York: Columbia University Press, 2014), 57–74.

256 Laxmi Prasad Pant and Helen Hambly Odame, "The promise of positive deviants: bridging divides between scientific research and local practices in smallholder agriculture," *Knowledge Management for Development Journal* 5, no. 2 (November 2009), 160–72, doi:10.1080/18716340903201504.

257 Author's interview with Zaccariah Nasreddin, mayor of al-Ain municipality, Lebanon, May 23, 2022.

258 Author's remote interview with UNDP official in Yemen, February 7, 2023.

259 Ahmad et al., "From dysfunctional to functional corruption," 7.

260 Author's remote interview with Federico Sittaro, strategic planner, International Committee of the Red Cross (ICRC), October 10, 2022.

261 Author's interview with EDL employee, Lebanon, May 26, 2022.

262 Cammett, "Positive deviance cases," 224–5.

263 Ibid.

264 Author's interview with IFI official working in Yemen, November 27, 2022.

265 Author's interview with Ammar al-Hayani, owner of Al-Taraib Solar, Baghdad, June 5, 2022.

266 Author's interview with Suha al-Kifaee, manager of International Islamic Bank, Baghdad, June 7, 2022.

267 "Giving countries in conflict their fair share of climate finance," International Crisis Group, November 1, 2022, https://www.crisisgroup.org/content/fair-share-of-climate-finance.

268 Chris Greacen, "Integrating Mini Grids into National Grids: Technical and Organizational Aspects," Nautilus Institute for Security and Sustainability, *NAPSNet Special Reports*, September 22, 2020, https://nautilus.org/napsnet/napsnet-special-reports/integrating-mini-grids-into-national-grids-technical-and-organizational-aspects/.

269 International Crisis Group, *Yemen's al-Qaeda: Expanding the Base* (Brussels: February 2017), Report No. 174, https://www.crisisgroup.org/middle-east-north-africa/gulf-and-arabian-peninsula/yemen/174-yemen-s-al-qaeda-expanding-base.

270 "Solar energy brings the power of sun to serve communities," YouTube video, posted by UNDP Yemen, November 15, 2021, 5:55, https://www.youtube.com/watch?v=c9nAIR271N4.

271 Ibid.